MW00462453

THE UNSEEN WORLD

Satan

VOLUME

3

OUR ADVERSARY THE DEVIL

Don
Stewart

Satan:
Our Adversary The Devil

© 2016 By Don Stewart

Published by EOW (Educating Our World)
www.educatingourworld.com
San Dimas, California 91773
All rights reserved

English Versions Cited

The various English versions which we cite in this course, apart from the King James Version, all have copyrights. They are listed as follows.

Verses marked NRSV are from the New Revised Standard Version, copyright 1989 by Division of Christian Education of the National Council of the Churches of Christ in the USA. Used by permission. All rights reserved

Verses marked NIV are taken from the HOLY BIBLE, New International Version 2011, Copyright 1973 1978, 1984, 2011 by International Bible Society. Used by permission of Zondervan Publishing House. All rights reserved

Verses marked ESV are from The Holy Bible English Standard Version™ Copyright © 2001 by Crossway Bibles, a division of Good News Publishers All rights reserved.

Scripture quotations marked (NLT) are taken from the Holy Bible, New Living Translation, copyright 1996. Used by permission of Tyndale House Publishers, Inc., Wheaton, Illinois 60189. All rights reserved.

Scripture quotations marked "NKJV" are taken from the New King James Version. Copyright © 1982 by Thomas Nelson, Inc. All rights reserved. Used by permission.

Scripture quotations marked CEV are taken from the Contemporary English Version (CEV) copyright American Bible Society 1991, 1995
Scripture quoted by permission. Quotations designated NET are from the NET Bible Copyright © 2003 By Biblical Studies Press, L.L.C. www.netbible.com All rights reserved.

Verses marked HCSB are taken from the Holman Christian Standard Bible® Copyright © 1999, 2000, 2002, 2003 by Holman Bible Publishers. Used by permission.

GOD'S WORD is a copyrighted work of God's Word to the Nations. Quotations are used by permission. Copyright 1995 by God's Word to the Nations. All rights reserved.

TABLE OF CONTENTS

Satan
Our Adversary The Devil

(Volume 3)

In the first volume of our series on the subject of the "Unseen World" we explored what the Bible had to say about the good angels. We found that they are created spirit-beings who are used in the service of the Lord. Their ministry is to believers only. We also discovered that there are other heavenly beings which the Lord has created which are distinct from the angels. They include the cherubim, seraphim, and the living creatures.

In the second book in our series we examined three separate topics with respect to the unseen world.

The first section dealt with the subject of evil angels. From the Bible we discovered that not all of the angels that exist today are good angels. We looked at the origin, current status, and destiny of the wicked angels.

In the next section, we considered the matter of demons. Where did they originate? What do they do? What victory do we have over them in Christ?

The last part of the book looked at a number of issues related to the occult. This included such things as talking with the dead and Halloween.

In our appendix we examined three often-asked questions about the unseen world. The first had to do with the Lord sending a "deceiving spirit" to King Ahab. The second question examined the question as to why the Lord sent an "evil spirit" to King Saul. The third question dealt with the identity of the "sons of God" in Genesis six.

Our third volume completes our study on the "Unseen World."

We will discover that there is a personage who exists who is the archenemy of God, and of humanity. He is known as Satan, the devil.

In this book we will consider the career of this evil being from his creation, fall, judgment, and final consignment to the lake of fire.

We will also consider how the believer can achieve victory in their life over this evil personage.

While we do not want to dwell on the subject of the devil, as Christians, there are certain things which we should know about him.

QUESTION 1

Does Satan, Or The Devil, Really Exist?

To many people, the idea of Satan, the devil, is nothing but a myth. He is a product of the imagination of superstitious people in a bygone age who did not know any better. We are often told that nobody in our modern world believes in the existence of a personal devil. Yet the Bible says that he is indeed a reality. The devil truly exists!

We can make the following observations about what the Bible has to say on this subject.

THE UNITED TESTIMONY OF SCRIPTURE SAYS HE EXISTS

From the Book of Genesis, through the Book of Revelation, the existence of an intelligent, cunning personage who is the great archenemy of humanity is taught.

Known by a number of different names, this personage is always treated as a real character. In fact, there is no indication whatsoever that he is merely a symbolic figure of evil.

In the Old Testament, Satan is referred to by name in two different books; Job, and Zechariah and likely in another book, 1 Chronicles. In the books of Genesis, Psalms, Ezekiel, and Isaiah, we seem to find Satan described, but with different names.

It is from the New Testament that we learn most of the things about him. Nineteen of the twenty-seven New Testament books refer to Satan.

They include: the Four Gospels, Acts, Romans, 1 and 2 Corinthians, Ephesians, 1 and 2 Thessalonians, 1 and 2 Timothy, Hebrews, James, 1 and 2 John, Jude, Revelation.

Therefore, we have a number of different authors, writing over a fifteen hundred year period, who testify to his existence. Were all of them mistaken when they wrote about this personage?

JESUS' TESTIMONY

In addition, we have the testimony of the Lord Jesus. Jesus acknowledged the existence of Satan. In fact, at least fifteen different times, and under five different names, Jesus asserted that the devil existed.

This personage had a confrontation with Jesus when the Lord was fasting during the period of His forty-day temptation. Matthew records it as follows.

> Then was Jesus led up of the Spirit into the wilderness to be tempted of the devil (Matthew 4:1 KJV).

On three different occasions in the temptation account, the Bible records the answers of Jesus to Satan. Obviously Christ was speaking to someone!

Also, five different times we find Jesus using personal pronouns when responding to the devil. To sum up, there is nothing in the temptation account that causes us to think that he is a mythological figure, or that Satan is merely a symbol of evil.

In fact, the Bible says that Jesus was alone in the wilderness when some personage arrived to tempt Him. If Christ was actually tempted, then He was tempted from someone apart from Himself. In other words, it was not by some evil principle that was within in.

Therefore, this personage who came to tempt Christ must be real. Otherwise, the temptation of Jesus makes no sense whatsoever.

PERSONAL PRONOUNS ARE USED OF HIM

Elsewhere, the Bible uses personal pronouns when describing Satan. This fact points unmistakably to an actual person. For example, the Lord spoke directly to Satan, and called him, "you." We read of this in the Book of Job.

> And the Lord said to Satan, "Have you considered my servant Job, that there is none like him on the earth, a blameless and upright man, who fears God and turns away from evil" (Job 1:8 ESV).

By speaking directly to Satan, and calling him "you," it shows that he is a real personage. Satan is also referred to with the pronouns "himself" and "you" in Job 2:2, as well as "you" in Zechariah 3:2. All of these uses are indications of personality.

HE HAS PERSONAL CHARACTERISTICS

Furthermore, personal characteristics are attributed to the devil. We can make the following observations.

1. SATAN HAS THE ABILITY TO ORGANIZE

The fact that the devil can organize his forces shows that he is a personal being. We read about this in the Book of Revelation.

> And war broke out in heaven; Michael and his angels fought against the dragon. The dragon and his angels fought back (Revelation 12:7 NRSV).

The dragon, who is identified as the devil, has a army of angels. This implies organization.

Later, we read in the Book of Revelation.

> When 1,000 years are over, Satan will be freed from his prison. He will go out to deceive Gog and Magog, the nations in the four corners of the earth, and gather them for war. They will be as numerous as the grains of sand on the seashore (Revelation 20:7,8 God's Word).

Again, we find this evil being organizing his forces. The ability of organize is a trait of personality; of a genuine being who exists.

There is also the inference in the Book of Ephesians that he is the head of an organized group of evil forces. Paul wrote.

> For we are not fighting against people made of flesh and blood, but against the evil rulers and authorities of the unseen world, against those mighty powers of darkness who rule this world, and against wicked spirits in the heavenly realms Ephesians 6:12 NLT).

This ability to organize evil forces is a trait of a personal being.

2. HE HAS KNOWLEDGE

When the devil is thrown down to the earth before the Second Coming of Jesus Christ, the Bible says that he knows his time is short. We read the following account in the Book of Revelation.

> Rejoice then, you heavens and those who dwell in them! But woe to the earth and the sea, for the devil has come down to you with great wrath, because he knows that his time is short! (Revelation 12:12 NRSV).

The devil knows who he is and that his time is limited. The fact that he has this knowledge reveals that he is a personal being.

Satan's servants, the demons, also know that their time is limited. Indeed, we find them acknowledging this when confronted with Jesus. Matthew writes.

> And behold, they cried out, "What have you to do with us, O Son of God? Have you come here to torment us before the time?" (Matthew 8:29 ESV).

If his servants know their time is limited, then certainly their master does also.

3. SATAN HAS INTELLIGENCE

Scripture tells us that Satan is able to form plans, use cunning, and deceive people. Paul spoke about the deceptive power of the serpent, the devil, when he wrote to the Corinthians. He stated it this way.

> But I am afraid that as the serpent deceived Eve by its cunning, your thoughts will be led astray from a sincere and pure devotion to Christ (2 Corinthians 11:3 NRSV).

Satan is able to form plans to deceive people. This is certainly a sign of intelligence.

4. HE CAN REASON

The fact that Satan quoted Scripture to the Lord Jesus during His forty-day temptation shows that he is a personal being. The Bible records the following.

> Then the devil took him into the holy city and had him stand on the highest part of the temple. He said to Jesus, "If you are the Son of God, jump! Scripture says, 'He will put his angels in charge of you. They will carry you in their hands so that you never hit your foot against a rock'" (Matthew 4:5,6 God's Word).

He was able to reason with Jesus by quoting an obscure verse of Scripture, out of context. This demonstrates intelligence, as well as cunning and deception.

5. HE HAS CHOICE OR A WILL

Satan has the power of choice. In the beginning, Scripture indicates that this created being chose to rebel against God, His Creator. We find that he has been making that same choice ever since. The Scripture, in speaking of him, says the following.

> You said in your heart, "I will ascend to heaven; I will raise my throne above the stars of God; I will sit enthroned on the mount of assembly, on the utmost heights of the sacred mountain. I will ascend above the tops of the clouds; I will make myself like the Most High" (Isaiah 14:13-14 NIV).

Choice is an obvious sign of personality.

6. SATAN HAS EMOTIONS

The Bible speaks of the devil showing emotions. He has shown the emotion of hatred for the things of God. Jesus said to Peter than Satan wanted to make demands upon him.

> Then the Lord said, "Simon, Simon, listen! Satan has demanded to have you apostles for himself. He wants to separate you from me as a farmer separates wheat from husks" (Luke 22:31 God's Word).

Satan can make demands. This means that he has emotions.

This evil being is also said to be conceited. Paul wrote.

> He must not be a recent convert, or he may become conceited and fall under the same judgment as the devil (1 Timothy 3:6 NIV).

The idea of the devil as being conceited fits the biblical picture of this personage. Indeed, he is a conceited arrogant being.

Among the emotions the devil shows is burning, or fierce, anger. We read of his wrath in the Book of Revelation.

> Be glad for this reason, heavens and those who live in them. How horrible it is for the earth and the sea because the Devil has come down to them with fierce anger, knowing that he has little time left (Revelation 12:12 God's Word).

The fact that he can exhibit burning anger is another indicator of emotion. This further demonstrates that the devil is a personal being.

7. HE HAS MEMORY

There is also the fact that Satan has memory. When tempting Jesus in the wilderness, he cited three different passages of Scripture. We should not assume that he had the written Scripture in front of him. Therefore, he cited the passages from memory. Only a genuine personage can have memory, not some mere symbol.

Each of these traits that are attributed to Satan are examples of one who has personality. In other words, he is a real person.

8. PERSONAL ACTIONS ARE ATTRIBUTED TO HIM

There are also personal actions attributed to the devil. They can be seen as follows.

A. HE IS ABLE TO TEMPT

The Bible calls Satan the "tempter." Matthew describes him this way.

> Then Jesus was led out into the wilderness by the Holy Spirit to be tempted there by the Devil (Matthew 4:1 NLT).

He attempted to cause Jesus to sin, but he failed in the task. He is, however, able to tempt people to sin. To be able to tempt shows intelligence and the ability to strategize. These are qualities of someone who is a personal being.

B. HE ACCUSES

The devil is able to accuse God's people. In fact, the Bible says that he accuses them day and night. John wrote the following in the Book of Revelation.

> Then I heard a loud voice in heaven, saying, "Now the salvation, power, kingdom of our God, and the authority of his Messiah have come. The one accusing our brothers and sisters, the one accusing them day and night in the presence of our God, has been thrown out" (Revelation 12:10 God's Word).

The ability to accuse is limited to personal beings.

The Old Testament also records accusations made by Satan. We read the following in the Book of Zechariah.

> Then he showed me Joshua the high priest standing before the angel of the Lord, and Satan standing at his right hand to accuse him (Zechariah 3:1 ESV).

As Joshua, the high priest, was a real person, so is Satan, his adversary.

C. HE CAN FIGHT

Satan is said to fight against God. His struggle is organized. This is another trait of personhood. The Book of Revelation says.

> And there was war in heaven: Michael and his angels fought against the dragon; and the dragon fought and his angels (Revelation 12:7 KJV).

We see a battle being waged between two armies. This fact shows that there is intelligence, and hence personality.

D. HE CAN COMMUNICATE

During the temptation of Jesus, Satan communicated to Him through the power of speech.

Also, in the Book of Job, Satan is also shown as talking to God. We read.

> Then Satan answered the LORD, "Does Job fear God for nothing? Have you not put a fence around him and his house and all that he has, on every side? You have blessed the work of his hands, and his possessions have increased in the land" (Job 1:9,10 NRSV).

Speech is only possible if Satan is a genuine personal being.

E. HE CAN PERFORM COUNTERFEIT SIGNS

Another trait of a genuine personality, which is found in Satan, is that his work consists of counterfeit signs performed through the coming man of sin, the final Antichrist. Paul wrote about this ability to perform counterfeit or false signs.

> The man of sin will come with the power of Satan. He will use every kind of power, including miraculous and wonderful signs. But they will be lies (2 Thessalonians 2:9 God's Word).

The fact that these counterfeit signs and wonders will be performed is further signs of personhood; for only a personal being could do something like this.

F. HE WILL BE PUNISHED

The fact that the devil will eventually be punished for his sins shows that he is more than a mere force or idea. The Book of Revelation explains his eventual fate.

And the devil who had deceived them was thrown into the lake of fire and sulfur, where the beast and the false prophet were, and they will be tormented day and night forever and ever (Revelation 20:10 NRSV).

You can only punish someone who is real. It is impossible to punish an idea or a symbol. Satan is a real being.

THE AUTHORITY OF SCRIPTURE IS AT STAKE

In sum, we find that the existence of a personal devil is tied to the issue of the authority of Scripture. If Scripture is accepted for what it claims to be, God's inspired Word, the final authority on all matters of faith and practice, then the existence of a personal devil is beyond all doubt.

However if one rejects, for whatever reason, the authority of Scripture with respect to the devil, then it is a short step to reject other important doctrines of Scripture. One cannot believe in a fully authoritative Scripture and, at the same time, reject its teaching about the existence and personality of the devil. To be consistent we must accept both.

SUMMARY TO QUESTION 1
DOES SATAN, THE DEVIL, REALLY EXIST?

The Bible does indeed teach the existence of a personal being known as the devil, or Satan. Satan is not a mere force, a symbolic figure of evil, or the figment of someone's imagination. He is a real personage. We discover this in the following ways.

First, Scripture always treats him as a personal being. Indeed, he is never describes as some impersonal force, or mere symbol of evil. In fact, in His dialogue with Satan, Jesus treated him as someone who has real substance. It is clear that the Lord was not having a discussing with some symbol.

We also find the devil in conversation with the Lord in the Book of Job. Again, there is every reason to believe that this is a report of something which actually happened. The fact that this personage is engaged in a conversation with the Lord testifies that he is a genuine being.

Furthermore, personal pronouns such as "he," "you," and "himself," are attributed to the devil. This is also consistent with the idea of a personal being.

In addition, he has the characteristics of one who has personality. Scripture says that he can think, choose, communicate and express emotions. Therefore, the characteristics which are attributed to him are all consistent with a personal being.

The devil has also performed certain actions which are consistent with personhood. The Bible says that he can tempt, accuse and fight. In fact, only a personal being could do these sorts of things which Scripture says that he does.

The Bible also says that there will come a day when the devil will be punished for his sin. Only a personal being can be punished in this manner, you cannot punish and idea or a symbol!

Finally, the existence and the personality of the devil is tied to the acceptance of the Scripture as God's revelation to humanity. If God's Word treats Satan as a real being then, to be consistent, so should we.

We conclude Satan is a genuine being that truly exists. There is no evidence whatsoever that we should understand him as some sort of illusion or symbol of evil.

QUESTION 2

Why Should We Study About Satan, The Devil?

If we grant that a personage named Satan does exist, why should the believer take any time to study about him? What are the reasons why Christians should desire to learn anything about this evil being?

Actually, there are a number of good reasons as to why we should study the subject of the devil. They include the following.

1. THE SUBJECT OF SATAN IS PART OF HOLY SCRIPTURE

To begin with, the subject of Satan, the devil, is part of Holy Scripture. The Bible testifies that all Scripture is profitable for study. Paul wrote.

> All scripture is inspired by God and is useful for teaching, for reproof, for correction, and for training in righteousness, so that everyone who belongs to God may be proficient, equipped for every good work (2 Timothy 3:16,17 NRSV).

Since all Scripture is profitable, and the subject of Satan, is part of Holy Scripture, it should be studied.

THE SUBJECT OF THE DEVIL MUST BE GIVEN THE PROPER EMPHASIS

However, while the subject of this personage should be studied, it should not be give undue emphasis.

For one thing, this character is found in various parts of Scripture but he is not "the" central character. Indeed, the Bible is all about God and humanity. It is the story of the living God and His dealings with the "human race." This should be the main focus of our study; we should never get sidetracked from it.

2. WE NEED TO KNOW WHO HE IS AND WHO HE IS NOT

It is also important that we know what the devil can, and cannot do. Unless we have the biblical perspective on the subject, we may attribute abilities to him that he does not have.

For example, a study of Scripture will demonstrate that he is not the opposite of God. Indeed, his powers are limited. While he is a powerful being, more powerful than any of us, we can defeat him through Jesus Christ.

The devil is a created being, created by God the Son, Jesus Christ. In other words, he has not always existed. This means his existence is dependent upon something other than himself. This is another illustration of the limitations that he has.

Since Satan is a created being, who was originally made perfect, this means that there has not been an eternal struggle of good versus evil, for evil has not always existed.

All of these things are important for us to understand.

3. WE NEED TO KNOW THAT HE HAS BEEN DEFEATED

It is also vital for believers to realize that Satan is a defeated foe. Jesus Christ has won the victory over Satan by His death on the cross of Calvary and His triumphal resurrection from the dead.

In fact, on the night that He was betrayed, Jesus said the following about the work of the Holy Spirit.

And when he comes, he will convict the world concerning sin and righteousness and judgment: concerning sin, because they do not believe in me; concerning righteousness, because I go to the Father, and you will see me no longer; concerning judgment, because the ruler of this world is judged (John 16:8-11 ESV).

The ruler of this world system, the devil, has indeed been judged.

This is crucial for us to realize. John would later write the following.

You are from God, little children, and you have conquered them, because the One who is in you is greater than the one who is in the world (1 John 4:4 HCSB).

The One in us, Jesus Christ, is greater than the one in this world, Satan. Jesus Christ has conquered the devil.

While believers have won the victory over him through Christ, the devil who knows this, still fights.

He also knows his time is running out and that nothing can stop this from happening. In fact, the Scripture says that he will ultimately end up in the lake of fire, punished there for all eternity.

Therefore, we need to look at the devil as a foe who has been defeated.

4. WE NEED TO KNOW HOW HE WORKS

Because Satan is the enemy of believers, it is necessary to know how he works. In fact, the Bible tells us that we should not be ignorant of the ways in which he operates. The Apostle Paul wrote the following.

So that Satan will not outsmart us. For we are very familiar with his evil schemes (2 Corinthians 2:11 NET).

Among other things, the Bible says that the devil plots and schemes against those people who believe in Jesus. He is clever. Believers need to be familiar with these evil schemes of the devil.

For example, we find that Satan can quote Scripture. In his temptation of Jesus Christ, we read the following.

"If you are the Son of God," he said, "throw yourself down. For it is written: "He will command his angels concerning you, and they will lift you up in their hands, so that you will not strike your foot against a stone" (Matthew 4:6 NIV).

As expected, the devil only partially cites what the Scripture says. In other words, he does not tell the full truth. This should warn us not accept someone merely because they can quote the Scripture. Indeed, the devil can do that.

In fact, he knows the Scripture from cover to cover. Yet he, and his ministers, only employ or use the Bible to misquote it. He wants people to be religious but he does not want them to believe in Jesus Christ!

5. WE CAN PREVENT TROUBLE FOR OURSELVES

If we do understand how Satan works, it will help us from getting into unnecessary trouble. In fact, often times, we can anticipate what he may do, and, therefore, we can avoid the problem.

Indeed, the Bible says that we are not to give him any opportunity to work in our lives. The Apostle Paul wrote.

Do not give the devil an opportunity (Ephesians 4:26 NET).

We are commanded not to give him any chance to cause trouble for us. This can only happen if we know how he works; and we can only discover this from a study of Scripture.

6. WE CAN CLEAR UP MISCONCEPTIONS ABOUT HIM

A biblical study of the subject of the devil can clear up a number of misconceptions that people hold. There is so much ignorance and misinformation about the subject of Satan.

For example, the Bible says that Satan is not in hell right now. Yet, many people wrongly assume this is the case. When the Bible is studied, we will discover that Satan is alive and working his evil plan here upon the earth. This misconception, about the devil being in hell, must be cleared up.

Neither does the Bible say that he is an ugly, hideous looking creature. Again, most people would probably assume this is what he is like. Yet the opposite is true. He always appears as a beautiful engaging creature. The devil never looks like what many people assume that he looks like.

7. WE NEED TO BE AWAKE!

In a parable that Jesus gave, He talked about the enemy sowing evil seed, or weeds, while the people were asleep.

> But that night as everyone slept, his enemy came and planted weeds among the wheat (Matthew 13:25 NLT).

The enemy did his work while people were sleeping. This is why we must be spiritually awake. When we understand what the Bible says, or does not say, we can have an accurate, though not complete, picture of the devil. This will keep us from giving him too much credit for things that occur, or in some cases, not enough credit.

8. AVOIDANCE OF THE SUBJECT IS WHAT SATAN PREFERS

Actually, Satan does not want people to believe that he exists. He would rather have them ignorant. In fact, the devil has truly succeeded when a person does not believe in his existence. Indeed, this is when his work of deception has been accomplished. If people believe that he is a mythical character, then he will be able to do much of his evil work unnoticed.

There is something else that must be understood. There is the fact that a particular man or woman may come to believe in the existence and the power of the devil but will not necessarily mean that he or she will believe in God. Satan can actually convince people to believe that he exists but that God does not!

However, once we are aware of what the Bible says about who he is, how he works, and what he can do and cannot do, then he can no longer work in ways that we are unaware of.

To sum up, God wants us to know some things about Satan while Satan wants us to be completely ignorant of who he is, and how he works.

THERE ARE TWO EXTREMES TO AVOID IN STUDYING THIS SUBJECT

There are two extremes that believers must avoid when we consider the subject of Satan. They are as follows.

WE SHOULD NOT IGNORE HIS EXISTENCE

First, it would be a mistake to ignore him entirely. He is real and he is our constant adversary. We are warned about him in Scripture and we are commanded not to be ignorant of the ways in which he works. It would be wrong to ignore him.

WE SHOULD NOT GIVE HIM TOO MUCH EMPHASIS

On the other hand, we should not give him too much credit. We do not want to make him out to be something that he is not. He is not the opposite of God. Indeed, he is not all-powerful, or all-knowing.

Neither can he harm believers without God's permission. Consequently, we do not want to have an unhealthy fascination with him. A balance is needed.

Two other points need to be made.

THERE IS NO SYMPATHY FOR THE DEVIL

Since this personage has chosen to rebel against God there should be no feeling of sorrow or sympathy toward him. He is a cunning, evil creature who wants to tempt, divide, and destroy God's people and God's work. He is completely dedicated to our downfall. We should hate him, not sympathize with him.

WE SHOULD BE CAREFUL OF SPECULATION ABOUT SATAN

Finally, the subject of Satan, the devil, has been revealed to us in Scripture. Therefore, it should be studied. However, it is not laid out for us in a systematic way in the Bible. There are some issues that are not as plain as we might like them to be.

For example, the origin of Satan is not clearly revealed to us. While Scripture seems to give us a good idea as to how he became the adversary of God and humanity, the information given to us about him is limited.

Consequently, we must be careful of the conclusions that we come to. There are other things about him that we are not told. When the Scriptures speak, then we speak. However, when they are silent, we must also be silent.

Therefore, it is best that we only say what the Bible says and nothing further. This is how we should treat this subject.

SUMMARY TO QUESTION 2
WHY SHOULD THE SUBJECT OF SATAN, OR THE DEVIL, BE STUDIED?

The Bible teaches the existence of a personal being known as Satan, the devil. Of this, there is no doubt.

Unfortunately, the subject of Satan is avoided by some believers, and is given too much emphasis by others. While some Christians do not wish to know anything about this personage, there are a number of reasons as to why we should know certain things about him. We can make the following observations.

While this is not a subject that Bible teachers and pastors enjoy teaching, nevertheless it needs to be taught. Like the topic of hell, the final punishment of the wicked, the issue of Satan should be dealt with.

Indeed, the subject of Satan is part of Holy Scripture and, therefore, must be taught because all Scripture is profitable for our instruction. It is not a subject which we should ignore.

In our study of Satan, we should only go as far as the Bible teaches. Consequently, we should not engage in fruitless speculation about his character. The key is to find the right balance. We need to know enough about our enemy so that we can understand how he works, but we should not be obsessed about him. In fact, our study of Scripture should concentrate on those things which Scripture itself emphasizes; the character of God and our relationship to Him.

In reality, our emphasis should always be on the Lord, not Satan because the Bible is all about the Him. It is not about the devil. In fact, the devil is only mentioned in Scripture when he has played some specific part in God's story of the salvation of humanity. Otherwise he is not mentioned at all.

Therefore, we should be careful not to speculate about this evil being. The key is to find the proper balance when looking into this subject.

In sum, when we study about the devil, and the various ways in which he works, it should always be in the context of studying about who God is, as well as His overall plan for the human race. This is where our energies should be directed.

What Does The Old Testament Have To Say About Satan?

It is important that we look at what the totality of Scripture has to say about Satan, the devil, to get a proper understanding of who he is, as well as the various ways in which he works.

To begin with, we need to look at what the Old Testament has to say about this personage. Interestingly, we will find that it actually does not give us too many specifics about this character. The evidence is as follows.

SATAN IN THE OLD TESTAMENT

The Hebrew word, *satan*, is transliterated as "Satan." This means that we have made an English word from the Hebrew letters and sounds. In other words, it is not a translation. The Hebrew word *satan* means "an adversary," or "one who resists."

Depending upon the context, it can be translated as "adversary" or it can be translated as a proper name, "Satan." In fact, eighteen times in the Old Testament we find this word transliterated as Satan and treated as a proper name in most Bible translations.

We also find that the word *satan* is used as both a noun and a verb. The instances of its use in the Old Testament are as follows.

THE VERB FORM OF THE HEBREW WORD SATAN IN THE OLD TESTAMENT

The verb, or participle form of *satan* is found a number of times in the Old Testament. For those who have forgotten their English grammar, a participle is a verbal adjective. It is formed from a verb but it can be used as an adjective or a noun. For example, we read in the psalms.

They repay me evil for the good I have done; though I have tried to do good to them, they hurl accusations at me (Psalm 38:20 NET).

The psalmist was being accused by others. "Hurl accusations" is the translation of the Hebrew word *satan*. It is used in the grammatical form of a participle.

In another place in the psalms, we read about other "accusers" of the psalmist. It says.

May my accusers be put to shame and consumed; with scorn and disgrace may they be covered who seek my hurt (Psalm 71:13 ESV).

"My accusers" is a translation of *satan*. In this verse, it is in the grammatical form of a participle.

The Hebrew verb *satan* is used three times in Psalm 104. It reads as follows.

In return for my friendship they accuse me, but I am a man of prayer . . . May this be the LORD's payment to my accusers, to those who speak evil of me. . . My accusers will be clothed with disgrace and wrapped in shame as in a cloak (Psalm 109:4,20,29 NIV).

Each time the word *satan* is translated by the word "accuse" or "accusers" This gives us further insight into the meaning of this term.

SATAN IS THE ACCUSER

In the Book of Zechariah we find another example of the verb form as well as the noun form of *satan*. It says the following.

Then he showed me Joshua the high priest standing before the angel of the Lord, and Satan standing at his right hand to accuse him (Zechariah 3:1 ESV).

Here the words "to accuse" is a translation of the Hebrew verb *satan*. We also find that the adversary, or Satan, is accusing Joshua the high priest. Therefore, in this verse the word is used as both a noun, translated "Satan" and a verb, translated "to accuse." Thus, the accuser is accusing.

Consequently, we find this word used in various contexts to refer to some type of adversary. In most of these cases it refers to some human adversary, but in the Book of Zechariah it is speaking of some non-human adversary, Satan, the devil.

THE NOUN FORM OF THE WORD SATAN

As mentioned, the Hebrew word *satan* is also used as a noun in the Old Testament. The uses can be seen as follows.

1. THE WORD SATAN IN THE BOOK OF JOB

Fourteen occurrences of the noun form of *satan* are found in the first two chapters of the Book of Job. In these chapters, "Satan" is making accusations to the Lord against the biblical character Job. English translations uniformly use the word "Satan" in these two chapters to describe this personage.

However, in each of these instances the word *satan* is preceded by the definite article "the." Consequently, some argue that instead of seeing this as a personal name, Satan, it could be translated as "the adversary."

2. SATAN IS REBUKED BY THE LORD IN ZECHARIAH

Another example where the word *satan* is used as a noun can be found in the Book of Zechariah. It reads as follows.

> Next I saw Joshua the high priest standing before the angel of the LORD, with Satan standing at his right hand to accuse him. The LORD said to Satan, "May the LORD rebuke you, Satan! may the LORD, who has chosen Jerusalem, rebuke you! Isn't this man like a burning stick snatched from the fire?" (Zechariah 3:1-2 NET).

In this passage, English translations uniformly use the word "Satan" in these verses to refer this personage. There seems to be no question that this is the same personage spoken of in the Book of Job.

As is the case in Job, the definite article precedes the word *satan*, therefore it could be translated "the adversary."

3. DAVID WAS INCITED BY SATAN TO NUMBER ISRAEL

There is another biblical reference that may, or may not, refer to the personage Satan. In the Book of Chronicles, we read that Satan incited David to take a census of Israel. We read the following words.

> Satan rose up against Israel and incited David to take a census of Israel (1 Chronicles 21:1 NIV).

However, the New English Translation uses the term "adversary" to describe the one who opposed Israel rather than assuming this is a proper name. It reads as follows.

> An adversary [*satan*] opposed Israel, inciting David to count how many warriors Israel had (1 Chronicles 21:1 NET).

In this instance, the Hebrew does not have the definite article in front of the word.

Therefore, it can be assumed to refer to "an" adversary in general rather than Satan, "the adversary" in particular. Consequently, there is some question in this context as to whether Satan himself is referred to, or merely some human adversary.

4. THE HEBREW WORD SATAN IS USED TO REFER TO HUMAN ADVERSARIES

It must be noted that the Hebrew word *satan* is used in some contexts to describe various humans who were adversaries of other humans.

For example, David is referred to as the "adversary," the Hebrew word satan, by the Philistines. We read about this in the Book of First Samuel.

> But the princes of the Philistines were angry with him; so the princes of the Philistines said to him, "Make this fellow return, that he may go back to the place which you have appointed for him, and do not let him go down with us to battle, lest in the battle he become our adversary [*satan*]. For with what could he reconcile himself to his master, if not with the heads of these men?" (1 Samuel 29:4 NKJV).

In this instance, David is their adversary.

Solomon had political enemies who were called his adversaries or *satan*. We read the following in First Kings.

> The LORD my God has now given me rest all around; there is no enemy or crisis (1 Kings 5:4 HCSB).

The "enemy" in this verse is called *satan*. Therefore, here we have an example of political enemies being the adversary, *satan*, of Solomon.

A man named Hadad the Edomite is called an adversary, or an enemy, of Solomon. Again it is the word satan which is used. Scripture says.

> So the LORD raised up Hadad the Edomite as an enemy against Solomon. He was of the royal family in Edom (1 Kings 11:14 HCSB).

This gives us further insight into the use of this term.

In another example in the days of Solomon, there was an adversary, or satan, named Rezon. We read in 1 Kings.

> God also raised up as an adversary to him, Rezon the son of Eliada, who had fled from his master Hadadezer king of Zobah. . . . He was an adversary of Israel all the days of Solomon, doing harm as Hadad did. And he loathed Israel and reigned over Syria (1 Kings 11:23,25 ESV).

Consequently, the word is used a number of times in the Old Testament to refer to human adversaries.

In sum, the Hebrew term can have the meaning of "adversary" without implying that a supernatural being is meant.

5. THE ANGEL OF THE LORD IS CALLED SATAN!

As we have already seen, the word *satan* may refer to non-human or supernatural adversaries. It all depends upon the context. However, these adversaries need not be evil personages.

Indeed, we find the angel of the Lord using the term *satan* to describe himself to the Gentile prophet Balaam! We read in the Book of Numbers.

> God's anger was kindled because he [Balaam] was going, and the angel of the LORD took his stand in the road as his adversary [satan]. Now he was riding on the donkey, and his two servants were with him. . . The angel of the LORD said to him, [Balaam] "Why have you struck your donkey these three times? I have come out as an adversary, [*satan*] because your way is perverse before me (Numbers 22:22,32 NRSV).

Obviously the word is not used here in any evil sense! Therefore, while the Hebrew word *satan* is used to describe various personages both human and non-human, these adversaries, *satan*, need not necessarily be looked upon as evil.

Consequently, it should not be assumed that when the Hebrew term *satan* is used in Scripture it automatically refers to this evil being called "the devil." It is not a technical term used exclusively of this wicked personage. Context must determine the identity of the adversary.

OTHER POSSIBLE OLD TESTAMENT REFERENCES TO SATAN OR THE DEVIL

While not mentioned by name, there are three other references in the Old Testament that seem to be referring to Satan, the devil. They are as follows.

SATAN IN THE GARDEN (GENESIS 3)

In the Garden of Eden, Eve is deceived by a serpent, a snake which is able to talk. While it is clear that an actual serpent, or snake, is in view, it seems from a study of the totality of Scripture the Satan, the devil was somehow speaking through the serpent or guiding his actions. In fact, there are hints of this in the Genesis account.

The Genesis creation account makes it clear that everything was created perfect on the earth. There was no evil anywhere. However, the serpent tempted Eve with evil. This means that the evil must have come from somewhere other than the perfect earth. Therefore, it seems logical to conclude that some other being, which was sinful at that time, was behind the actions of the serpent.

It is important to note that Moses, the writer of Genesis, did not identify the serpent with any other being. Neither does the rest of the Old Testament. Read on its own, it would seem that the serpent alone is held responsible for tempting Adam and Eve. However, what is not answered is the issue of how this beast could tempt humanity with evil when the world was still perfect.

It is from the New Testament we discover that the personage behind the deeds of the serpent was the devil himself. In some way, unknown and unexplained to us, the serpent was used by the devil to tempt Adam and Eve.

Therefore, from the Genesis story of Adam and Eve there is no statement of the existence of such a person as the devil but what is told about the tempter is certainly consistent with the remainder of Scripture which speaks of a personal devil who works his evil in this world.

THE KING OF BABYLON (ISAIAH 14)

In the Book of Isaiah, there is judgment pronounced against the King of Babylon. The description of this earthly king does not seem to fit a mere human being. This personage is called "son of dawn," or "morning star." This passage records this being saying, "I will ascend to heaven," "I will raise my throne above the stars of God and "I will make myself like the Most High."

This appears to be describing someone other than an earthly creature. Therefore, it is widely believed that Isaiah is describing the fall of the created being who became Satan in this passage. Yet there are those who do not necessarily see this as a reference to the fall of Satan.

THE KING OF TYRE (EZEKIEL 28)

There is also judgment pronounced against the King of Tyre as recorded in the Book of Ezekiel. While referring initially to an earthly ruler, the description seems to be going beyond a mere earthly personage. He is said to be "perfect in beauty," and the "anointed cherub." It is also said of him that "he was on the holy mountain" and "he was blameless." Since this can hardly describe an earthly, pagan ruler, many think that Satan, the devil, is ultimately in view.

While there is no mention of the name Satan in these three passages, nor do they specifically speak of a non-human created being, they do seem to be referring to some created being who existed with God in the beginning and eventually became the devil.

If not, we would apparently have to assume that God created this being as sinful. However, the Bible makes it clear that everything God created was created "very good."

Consequently, it seems that we can be somewhat certain that these passages also refer to this spirit-being who was created perfect but then became Satan, the Adversary.

To sum up, we know that the devil became evil, though we may not be entirely certain how this occurred. To conclude that Satan is the personage behind the serpent in Genesis chapter three, as well as the King of Babylon in Isaiah, and the King of Tyre in the Book of Ezekiel, is consistent with the rest of Scripture, though nothing is specifically said in these passages which identifies him as a perfect created being who fell from his original state.

THE TERM DEVIL IS NOT FOUND IN THE OLD TESTAMENT

What we do know for certain is while the term *satan* is used in the Old Testament to describe this personage, the word devil, which means "slanderer," is not found in the Old Testament; it is a New Testament term.

SATAN'S BEHAVIOR IN THE OLD TESTAMENT

There is not much in the Old Testament to give us an understanding of the behavior of Satan. Our first introduction to Satan, the adversary, is in the Book of Job. Interestingly, in Job, he is Job's adversary, not God's.

In the Book of Job, Satan asks God for a number of things that he might do to Job. In fact, he does not demand anything from God. God allows Satan to do limited things to Job. Satan always follows the commands that God gives him. In other words, he acts at God's direction without disobeying him.

Therefore, what we learn about Satan in the first two chapters of the Book of Job, is that he is Job's adversary, but we are not told that he is the adversary of every human being. This truth is not revealed in the Book of Job itself.

In the Book of Zechariah, he is more of a potential accuser than an actual accuser. He is ready to accuse Joshua the High Priest but he is rebuked by the Lord. There is nothing specifically said in this context that he accuses all believers.

In fact, apart from his identification as an "accuser," there is nothing specific which links him to the personage in the Book of Job though it does seem relatively certain both passages are speaking about the same figure.

In the instance of David numbering the people of Israel, Satan, the adversary, is the one who incites David to commit this sin. Whether it is Satan himself, or some human adversary, we are not certain. However, David, and David alone, is ultimately held responsible for his sin.

CONCLUSION ON OLD TESTAMENT TEACHING ON SATAN

In sum, from what the Old Testament specifically says about Satan we find that he is an adversary. However, he is not portrayed as an adversary of God, or even of all humans.

He is a heavenly being who is the adversary of Job, and the potential adversary of Joshua the High Priest. He also may be the one who incited King David to number the men of Israel. Obviously, there are not very many specifics given to us about him.

It is from the New Testament that we learn that he is the enemy of all humanity. In fact, the New Testament gives us a clearer picture of this personage who is only somewhat revealed in the Old Testament.

SUMMARY TO QUESTION 3
WHAT DOES THE OLD TESTAMENT HAVE TO SAY ABOUT SATAN?

The Old Testament does not provide us with a lot of information about Satan, the devil. It does speak of a personal being known as Satan, the adversary. This adversary is spoken of in the Book of Job, and the Book Zechariah. These references seem to be speaking of the same personage. There is a reference to an adversary in the Book of Chronicles but the identity of this adversary is not certain.

Moreover, we find that the Hebrew noun and verb *satan* is not a technical term for this evil personage. In the Old Testament humans, as well as the angel of the Lord, are called "satan," the adversary. Context must determine whether the adversary is good or evil. Therefore, this is a neutral term.

Three other passages in the Old Testament seem to be referring to this personage known as Satan, the devil.

The narrative of the fall of humanity in the Garden of Eden describes a being called the serpent. The serpent, which was able to speak, used his craftiness to tempt Eve to sin. While he is often identified with Satan he is not called anything other than a snake in the Genesis account, or anywhere else in the Old Testament.

Yet, it seems that for temptation to come to a perfect world it must have had its origin outside of the world. Therefore, it is consistent to conclude that some outside being influenced the serpent to tempt Eve in some unexplained way.

In the Book of Isaiah, there is judgment spoken of against the king of Babylon. It seems from the description given that we are dealing with more than an earthly king. Certain features are attributed to him that would not be possible for a human being to have. However, not all Bible students see this as a reference to Satan.

Likewise, in the Book of Ezekiel, we have a description of the judgment against the earthly king of Tyre. While some of the descriptions can be referring to an earthly king, a number of things said about him seem to be describing another personage.

Again, it is often assumed that this is a description of the fall of the created being who became Satan, the adversary. This does fit with the rest of Scripture. It says that God created everything perfect in the beginning; this, of course, would include this supernatural creature who became the adversary, Satan.

From the Old Testament, we find that Satan does not appear as God's adversary or enemy. He is Job's accuser in the Book of Job and a potential accuser of Joshua the High Priest in Zechariah. Beyond that, nothing is said.

In sum, the Old Testament does not contain much information about him or his actions. However, from the New Testament, there is a much greater amount of information that builds upon that which has been revealed in the Old Testament. In point of fact, most of the truths we know about this personage are found in the New Testament.

What Do The Four Gospels Have To Say About Satan?

The Old Testament introduces us to a personage called Satan, the adversary. In the Book of Job, this character makes accusations about Job before the Lord.

In the Book of Zechariah, he desired to accuse Joshua the High Priest, but was rebuked from doing so.

There is also a possible reference to him inciting David to number the people of Israel. Beyond this, he is possibly referred to as the personage behind the serpent in Genesis three, the king of Babylon in Isaiah, and the king of Tyre in the Book of Ezekiel. As we can observe, not that much is said about this being.

THE NEW TESTAMENT HAS MUCH TO SAY ABOUT SATAN

However, this is certainly not the case in the New Testament. The Greek word *satanas*, transliterated as Satan, occurs thirty-six times in the New Testament. In this question, we will examine what the four gospels have to say with respect to this personage known as "Satan."

SATAN IN THE FOUR GOSPELS

The word *satan* is found about eighteen times in the four gospels. He is also referred to as "the devil," and the "evil one." The evidence is as follows.

1. SATAN TEMPTED JESUS FOR FORTY DAYS IN THE WILDERNESS

We first meet Satan at the temptation of Jesus. Each of the first three gospels mentions him as the one who tempted the Lord. For example, we read.

> The Spirit immediately drove him into the wilderness. He was in the wilderness forty days, enduring temptations from Satan (Mark 1:12 NET).

Three separate temptations from the devil are recorded in gospels. He wanted Jesus to turn stones into bread, to jump safely from the pinnacle of the temple before a large crowd, and to fall down and worship him. Jesus refused on each of these occasions. We are then told that Satan left him for a little while.

2. THE BEELZEBUB CONTROVERSY

We find Satan mentioned again by Jesus when confronting the religious leaders. Jesus made the following comment.

> And if Satan is casting out Satan, he is fighting against himself. His own kingdom will not survive (Matthew 12:26 NLT).

Jesus said this in response to the charge that Satan was actually energizing Him. The Lord made it clear that His intention was to drive out Satan.

3. THE INFIRMED WOMAN

On another occasion, Jesus healed an infirmed woman whom He said had been bound by Satan. He described her in this manner.

> Satan has bound this woman, a daughter of Abraham, for 18 years—shouldn't she be untied from this bondage on the Sabbath day (Luke 13:16 HCSB).

This woman is described as having been kept bound by Satan for some eighteen years.

4. SATAN FALLING FROM HEAVEN

Jesus sent out seventy disciples, or seventy-two disciples (there is a variant reading in the text), with power over the unclean spirits. They returned and testified to the power they had over everything. The Bible says.

> The seventy-two returned with joy, saying, "Lord, even the demons are subject to us in your name!" And he said to them, "I saw Satan fall like lightning from heaven" (Luke 10:17,18 ESV).

This statement seems to speak of the authority of Satan being greatly diminished or lost. Indeed, as this select group of people went through Israel preaching the message about Jesus it became obvious that Christ had absolute authority over Satan and his demonic realm.

WAS JESUS REFERRING TO THE ORIGINAL FALL OF THIS PERSONAGE?

Some Bible students believe that Jesus may have been referring to Isaiah's description of the fall of Satan from heaven. He wrote the following words.

> How you have fallen from heaven, O morning star, son of the dawn! You have been cast down to the earth, you who once laid low the nations (Isaiah 14:12 NIV).

However, this passage in Luke seems to be a reference to the eventual demise of Satan. We know that this event is still in the future.

5. SATAN OPPOSES THE PROCLAMATION OF THE GOSPEL

We are told that Satan opposes the proclamation of the gospel, or good news, of Christ. In the parable of the sower, Mark records Jesus saying the following about what happens when seed is sown.

And these are the ones along the path, where the word is sown: when they hear, Satan immediately comes and takes away the word that is sown in them (Mark 4:15 ESV).

In the parallel passages in Matthew and Luke, we find that they each use different terms to describe Satan.

In Matthew, he is called the "evil one."

When anyone hears the word about the kingdom and does not understand it, the evil one comes and snatches what was sown in his heart; this is the seed sown along the path (Matthew 13:19 NET).

Therefore, Matthew uses a different description to describe the same personage.

In Luke, another term is used. He is called "the devil." The Bible says.

Those along the path are the ones who have heard; then the devil comes and takes away the word from their hearts, so that they may not believe and be saved (Luke 8:12 NET).

This demonstrates that this evil personage, Satan, has a number of different titles, or names, that are ascribed to him.

6. SATAN INFLUENCED PETER TO HAVE JESUS BYPASS THE CROSS

We also find that Satan influenced Simon Peter. When Jesus told His disciples that He was going to die on the cross, Peter rebuked Him. Jesus, in turn, rebuked Peter for his words. Matthew records what took place.

But he turned and said to Peter, "Get behind me, Satan! You are a stumbling block to me, because you are not setting your mind on God's interests, but on man's" (Matthew 16:23 NET).

The idea that Jesus was to bypass the cross was a satanic idea. Indeed, this was the reason that Christ came into the world. In fact, later in the gospel of Matthew the Lord would make this clear. He put it this way.

> Just as the Son of Man did not come to be served, but to serve, and to give His life—a ransom for many (Matthew 20:28 HCSB).

Christ came to earth to serve others and eventually to die for the sins of the world. Therefore, any suggestion that Jesus alter the reason that He came into the world was a satanic idea.

7. SATAN'S DESIRE TO SIFT THE DISCIPLES

Jesus said that Satan desired to sift all of the disciples like wheat. He warned Peter about the intentions of this evil personage.

> Simon, Simon, Satan has asked to have all of you, to sift you like wheat (Luke 22:31 NLT).

The exact meaning of this warning is not certain. Whatever it did mean, it was obviously something that would be to their disadvantage.

8. SATAN ENTERED JUDAS ISCARIOT

We are told that Satan entered Judas on the night that he betrayed Jesus. John wrote about this occurring. He said.

> And after Judas took the piece of bread Satan entered into him. Jesus said to him, "What you are about to do, do quickly" (John 13:27 NET).

John testified that Satan had the capability of entering another human being. In this instance, it was one of Jesus' own disciples.

We read in Luke's gospel what happened next. We find that after Satan entered Judas, he went to the priests and betrayed the Lord Jesus.

Then Satan entered Judas, the one called Iscariot, who was one of the twelve. He went away and discussed with the chief priests and officers of the temple guard how he might betray Jesus, handing him over to them (Luke 22:3,4 NET).

Judas allowed Satan to enter into him and, therefore, he went to the chief priests to betray Jesus.

9. SATAN HAS BEEN JUDGED

Jesus said that Satan, the ruler of this world, has been judged. While with His disciples, shortly before His betrayal, He said the following about the devil.

The ruler of this world is judged (John 16:11 ESV).

Note that Jesus called him the "ruler of this world. Satan has been judged by the coming of Jesus into the world. Indeed, His sinless life, death on the cross, and triumphal resurrection from the dead assured Satan's defeat.

This is a brief summation of what the four gospels have to say about Satan.

SUMMARY TO QUESTION 4
WHAT DO THE FOUR GOSPELS HAVE TO SAY ABOUT SATAN?

From the Old Testament, we learn of the existence of a being known as Satan. While not much is taught about him there are a few things which we can learn.

In the Old Testament, he is seen as accusing the patriarch Job, as well as desiring to accuse Zechariah the High Priest. He does not act as God's adversary but rather as an enemy of certain of God's people. While he is mentioned in the Old Testament, there is not much information about him, or his evil deeds.

It is the New Testament which adds greatly to our knowledge of Satan. In fact, most of what we know about him comes from the New Testament, especially the four gospels.

To begin with, we find that this evil personage tempted Jesus Christ for a forty day period. After that, he left Jesus for a short time.

During His public ministry, Jesus specifically mentioned Satan, the devil, or the evil one, on a number of occasions.

For example, we are told by Jesus that an infirmed woman had been bound by Satan for some eighteen years before the Lord healed her.

In another instance, we find that the disciples of Jesus were given power of Satan and his demonic underlings.

The Bible also says that Satan entered Judas on the night he betrayed the Lord. On that same night, Jesus proclaimed that Satan has been defeated.

Consequently throughout the earthly ministry of Jesus, we find this evil personage attempting to thwart the plan of God. As the four gospels so clearly state, this personage miserably failed in his attempts. Indeed, Jesus Christ is the victor over Satan in all things!

What Does The Bible Tell Us About Satan Outside Of The Old Testament And The Four Gospels?

We have discovered that the Old Testament tells us certain things about this being known as Satan, the adversary. In addition, we learn a great deal more about this personage from the four gospels.

We now turn to the remainder of the New Testament where will find further information about this evil being.

THE BOOK OF ACTS

In the New Testament, Satan is mentioned outside of the four gospels. For example, in the Book of Acts, he is encountered on the following occasions.

1. SATAN FILLED THE HEART OF ANANIAS

The Bible says that Satan filled the heart of a certain disciple named Ananias to sin against the Lord. The Bible records it as follows.

> But Peter said, "Ananias, why has Satan filled your heart to lie to the Holy Spirit and keep back for yourself part of the proceeds from the sale of the land?" (Acts 5:3 NET).

Like Judas, Satan entered the heart of Ananias to do something evil. In this instance, he lied to the Holy Spirit.

2. JESUS HEALED THOSE OPPRESSED BY THE DEVIL

Peter, in speaking of the earthly ministry of Jesus, said that He healed those whom the devil had oppressed.

> And no doubt you know that God anointed Jesus of Nazareth with the Holy Spirit and with power. Then Jesus went around doing good and healing all who were oppressed by the Devil, for God was with him (Acts 10:38 NLT).

Jesus set these people free from their oppression. He is still doing the same thing today.

3. UNBELIEVERS WENT FROM THE CONTROL OF SATAN TO THE CONTROL OF GOD

When Saul of Tarsus was converted to the Apostle Paul, the Lord said the following to him about his future ministry.

> I will rescue you from the Jewish people and from the non-Jewish people to whom I am sending you. You will open their eyes and turn them from darkness to light and from Satan's control to God's. Then they will receive forgiveness for their sins and a share among God's people who are made holy by believing in me (Acts 26:17,18 God's Word).

Those who believe in Jesus Christ are freed from the control of Satan so they can now serve the Lord. They have turned from the darkness and have come into the light.

THE MENTION OF SATAN IN THE NEW TESTAMENT LETTERS

Apart from the mention of Satan in the historical examples in the gospels and Acts, he is also referred to in the New Testament letters. We discover the following things.

1. SATAN OPPOSES GOD'S WORK

The Apostle Paul wrote to the Thessalonians and reported how Satan was opposing the work of God. He wrote.

> For we wanted to come to you (I, Paul, in fact tried again and again) but Satan thwarted us (1 Thessalonians 2:18 NET).

Satan attempted to stop the Lord working through His people here upon the earth. Ultimately, he cannot succeed.

2. SATAN HINDERS THE MESSAGE OF THE GOSPEL

We are also told that this evil being hinders the preaching of the message of the gospel of Jesus Christ. Paul wrote the following to the believers in Corinth.

> If the Good News we preach is veiled from anyone, it is a sign that they are perishing. Satan, the god of this evil world, has blinded the minds of those who don't believe, so they are unable to see the glorious light of the Good News that is shining upon them. They don't understand the message we preach about the glory of Christ, who is the exact likeness of God (2 Corinthians 4:3,4 NLT).

Note that Paul says that there is a satanic blindfold over the eyes of those who do not believe. Therefore, they cannot understand the message of Christ until this blindfold has been removed. In sum, Satan does not want unbelievers to see the light of Jesus Christ. Indeed, he wants to keep them in spiritual darkness.

3. HE IS ABLE TO DO LYING WONDERS

Satan, we are told, can do deceptive signs and wonders. Paul wrote.

> The coming of the lawless one is by the activity of Satan with all power and false signs and wonders (2 Thessalonians 2:9 ESV).

These deceptive signs are meant to lead people astray. Among other things, this informs us that we are not to follow someone merely because they can perform miracles. Indeed, there are such things as bogus signs and wonders.

4. PAUL TURNED A SINNING BELIEVER OVER TO SATAN

The Apostle Paul ordered the church at Corinth to turn a sinning brother over to Satan. He wrote the following.

> When you have gathered together, I am with you in spirit. Then, in the name of our Lord Jesus, and with his power, hand such a person over to Satan to destroy his corrupt nature so that his spiritual nature may be saved on the day of the Lord (1 Corinthians 5:4-5 God's Word).

This sinning person was to be turned over to Satan. However, this was something only temporary. His spirit was still to be saved.

5. A MESSENGER OF SATAN TRIED TO STOP PAUL

The Apostle Paul said that a messenger of Satan was sent to stop him. He said the following to the Corinthians.

> Even because of the extraordinary character of the revelations. Therefore, so that I would not become arrogant, a thorn in the flesh was given to me, a messenger of Satan to trouble me—so that I would not become arrogant (2 Corinthians 12:7 NET).

This messenger was called a "thorn in the flesh."

6. SATAN COMES AS AN ANGEL OF LIGHT

We are told that Satan appears as an angel of light. Paul wrote about this aspect of Satan to the Corinthians. He said.

For such people are false apostles, deceitful workers, disguising themselves as apostles of Christ. And no wonder! For Satan himself is disguised as an angel of light (2 Corinthians 11:13-14 HCSB).

He appears as a beautiful creature; one that does not look the way in which we would expect him to look. In other words, he fools us with his appearance and with the clever things he says.

7. SATAN WILL BE HURLED TO THE EARTH

In the Book of Revelation we find that Satan will be thrown out of heaven down to the earth along with his evil angels. John said.

So the great dragon was thrown out—the ancient serpent, who is called the Devil and Satan, the one who deceives the whole world. He was thrown to earth, and his angels with him (Revelation 12:9 HCSB).

Eventually, this wicked being will be thrown out of heaven with his evil angels.

8. SATAN'S FINAL PUNISHMENT

Satan will be punished along with two other personages, the beast and the false prophet. They will be sent to the Lake of Fire. The Bible says.

And the devil who deceived them was thrown into the lake of fire and sulfur, where the beast and the false prophet are too, and they will be tormented there day and night forever and ever (Revelation 20:10 NET).

Scripture says he will spend eternity apart from the Lord. He will be consciously punished for his rebellion against the God of the Bible.

These are the things that the New Testament tells us about Satan, the devil. From it, we can have an accurate picture, though not a complete one, of this enemy of God and humanity.

SUMMARY TO QUESTION 5
WHAT DOES THE BIBLE TELL US ABOUT SATAN OUTSIDE OF THE OLD TESTAMENT AND THE FOUR GOSPELS?

The four gospels tell us that Satan tried to thwart the ministry of Jesus. In doing so, he miserably failed. However, this did not stop him. Indeed, we find that he was also active after the life and ministry of Jesus.

In the Book of Acts we find that Satan filled the heart of a believer named Ananias to lie to the apostles.

Peter, in preaching to the Gentiles, emphasized that Jesus had healed those who had been "oppressed" by the devil. This oppression by the devil was still continuing after Jesus' earthly ministry was completed.

The Lord told Saul of Tarsus, who became the Apostle Paul, that he was specially designated by Christ to preach the gospel. This message about Jesus would free people from the power of Satan. This further illustrates the biblical teaching that the devil is keeping individuals bound in sin.

In the New Testament letters, we find this personage further mentioned. The Apostle Paul told the Thessalonians that Satan hindered him from coming to see the believers in that city.

In addition, Paul wrote to the Thessalonians that Satan does lying signs and wonders in order to deceive people. In other words, counterfeit miracles can proceed from him.

Finally, in the Book of Revelation, we are told that Satan will eventually be sent to the Lake of fire where he will be consciously tormented forever and ever.

In sum, we discover that in every reference to Satan in the New Testament he is treated as an evil personal being whose existence is taken for granted.

QUESTION 6

What Is The Career Of Satan?

To understand the identity of Satan, the devil, we must take a general look at his career. There are a number of stages in which we can trace his inglorious history, to his well-deserved destiny. From the evidence of both testaments, we can make the following summary statements about this evil personage.

1. HIS POSITION BEFORE HIS FALL

The origin of Satan is unclear. Indeed, the teaching in Scripture is not direct. What does seem clear is that there was a time when this created being was in an unfallen, sinless state. At that time, he, along with the rest of creation, was in one accord with God. Scripture describes him as a high-ranking created being, perhaps even the highest. However, the Bible does not tell us his name.

What we can say is this: there is no hint in Scripture that the Lord created this personage as an evil being. The holy, righteous God of the Bible could not have created anything that was evil in its nature.

In fact, the Bible tells us that when God created everything on this earth He created it "very good."

> God saw all that he had made, and it was very good. And there was evening, and there was morning—the sixth day (Genesis 1:31 NIV).

The same would hold true about His creation of this being who became Satan.

2. THE FALL OF SATAN

At some time in the dateless past, this particular created being seems to have decided to rebel against God. Lifted up with pride and selfish ambition, he took a large number of angels with him when he rebelled. The Scripture speaks of these "angels that sinned." Peter wrote.

> For God did not spare even the angels when they sinned; he threw them into hell, in gloomy caves and darkness until the judgment day (2 Peter 2:4 NLT).

This personage would be included in this group of beings who sinned against the Lord. However, it seems that he was created above the angels. In other words, he was in a higher category of created beings. Therefore, technically it is probably not correct to call him an "angel."

3. THE JUDGMENT-LOSS OF FAVORED POSITION

When this occurred, this created being lost the favored position that he had with the Lord. He was now Satan, the "adversary." This seems to be the best way of understanding what the totality of Scripture has to say on the subject.

4. SIN ENTERS OUR WORLD

What we do know for certain is this: this personage, who became Satan, is now seen as a fallen being. What we also know for certain is that since the time of his fall, the devil has attempted to deceive humanity. In doing so, he has been given limited powers by God. His main goal is to turn people away from the worship and service of the Lord.

In fact, we find him appearing in the Garden of Eden in the form of a serpent. Genesis chapter three informs us that he tempted Adam and Eve to sin. His temptation succeeded, and sin entered the previously perfect world.

5. HE WAS DEFEATED BY CHRIST

As soon as sin entered into our world, the Lord promised to send someone to deal with the problem, a Savior, a Deliverer. Two thousand years ago, the promise became a reality. Indeed, God the Son became a human being in the person of Jesus Christ.

Satan attempted to thwart the mission of Christ, but it was without any success. The devil was defeated by the Lord; at the cross and then by His resurrection from the dead.

6. HIS PRESENT POSITION IS TO DECEIVE HUMANITY

Presently we are in an interval period between the two comings of Christ. Satan is continuing to deceive humanity, as he has done from the beginning. He never ceases from his evil work.

7. HE WILL BE THROWN DOWN TO THE EARTH

In the next step in his judgment, Satan will be thrown out of heaven, and sent down to the earth. This will happen before the Second Coming of Christ.

8. HE WILL BE PLACED IN THE BOTTOMLESS PIT

When Jesus Christ returns, Satan will be bound and placed in the bottomless pit, the abyss, for a thousand years.

9. HE WILL BE RELEASED FOR A SHORT TIME

At the end of the thousand years, he will be released for a short period of time. Then he will deceive the people for one last time.

After this last deception of humanity, Satan, the devil, will be once-and-for-all finished with his efforts to bring sin in our universe.

10. SATAN WILL BE THROWN INTO THE LAKE OF FIRE

At the Great White Throne judgment, he will be thrown into the lake of fire. There he will be punished forever and ever. This will be his ultimate destiny.

Therefore, the career of Satan has been going in one direction, down. From an exalted place next to God Himself, he will eventually end up in the Lake of fire. His path to destruction is certainly a pathetic one.

SUMMARY TO QUESTION 6
WHAT IS THE CAREER OF SATAN?

While there is much about Satan, the devil, that we do not know, we apparently can have a general idea of his career. This includes the following facts.

Satan, the devil, it seems, was a created being who was perfect in all his ways. In fact, it seems that he may have had the position of the highest created being that the Lord God had made. Like everything else in God's universe this personage was without sin of any type.

Yet, at a certain point in the dateless past, this perfect being decided to rebel against God. When this occurred, he brought sin into the perfect universe. Consequently he was judged for that sin and lost his favored position with God. He became "the devil," or "the adversary."

The Bible says that Satan has tempted humanity as long as the human race has existed. Adam, and Eve, the first humans, succumbed to his temptation, which was given through the form an earthly creature, a serpent. In doing so, they brought sin into this world by their disobedience.

The good news is that sin and Satan were defeated by Jesus' sinless life, His death on the cross, and His resurrection from the dead. Jesus made it clear that His death was a defeat for the devil and a victory for God.

Although Satan continues to deceive humanity, his ultimate doom is sealed. He will be thrown down to the earth before the Second Coming of Christ. At Christ's return he will be placed in a bottomless pit.

Eventually, after the end of the thousand year reign of Christ upon the earth, he will be released from that pit to deceive the nations one last time.

After that event, there is the final judgment, where he will be thrown into the lake of fire. There he will remain forever in a state of constant punishment. This ends his inglorious career.

How Is Satan's Character Described?

What do we know of the character of Satan? How does the Bible describe him? From Scripture, we have the following things said of Satan's character.

1. HE IS FIERCE AND CRUEL

The devil is described as being fierce and cruel. In fact, Peter likens him to a lion which walks around looking for anyone to devour.

> Be sober! Be on the alert! Your adversary the Devil is prowling around like a roaring lion, looking for anyone he can devour (1 Peter 5:8 HCSB).

The picture of Satan, as a hungry lion, should certainly get our attention!

It is interesting to note that Jesus is also compared to a lion. The Book of Revelation says the following of the glorified Christ.

> But one of the twenty-four elders said to me, "Stop weeping! Look, the Lion of the tribe of Judah, the heir to David's throne, has conquered. He is worthy to open the scroll and break its seven seals" (Revelation 5:5 NLT).

While the lion is used to symbolize both Jesus and Satan, there are obviously different characteristics of the lion that are emphasized in these two descriptions.

2. THE DEVIL IS POWERFUL

The devil is a powerful being. Even Michael the archangel would not rebuke him without calling upon the name of the Lord. We read about this in Jude. It says.

> But when the archangel Michael contended with the devil and disputed about the body of Moses, he did not dare to bring a condemnation of slander against him, but said, "The Lord rebuke you!" (Jude 9 NRSV).

This gives us some insight into his power. He is not to be trifled with. Indeed, he is an extremely powerful evil being.

3. SATAN IS DECEITFUL

Satan's methods consist of deception. Paul wrote to the Ephesians about standing firm against the schemes of this creature.

> Put on the whole armor of God, that you may be able to stand against the schemes of the devil (Ephesians 6:11 ESV).

The Bible makes it clear that the devil deceives and schemes. He wants to confuse people. This is how he operates.

4. OUR ENEMY IS CUNNING

He is also described as cunning. Paul wrote to the Corinthians about this aspect of Satan's character.

> But I am afraid that as the serpent deceived Eve by its cunning, your thoughts will be led astray from a sincere and pure devotion to Christ (2 Corinthians 11:3 NRSV).

Satan is a cunning creature. This should serve as warning to everyone. The devil is an intelligent, cunning being. In fact, he is more intelligent than we are. We cannot outsmart him. However, what we can do is to be aware of the tricks he uses.

5. THIS EVIL BEING CONDEMNS BELIEVERS

Satan is described as one who condemns those who believe in Jesus. Paul gave the following warning to Timothy about those who want to be elders in the church.

> He must not be a new convert, or he might become conceited and fall into the condemnation of the Devil (1 Timothy 3:6 HCSB).

The devil wants to condemn us. Indeed, he wants to discourage us from serving the Lord. This evil personage will use any method which he can to do this.

6. HE WANTS US TO FOCUS UPON OUR FAILURES

One of the ways in which Satan condemns people is that he wants us to think about the various failures in our lives. Each of us has failed time after time. The devil wants us to focus upon these failures. If he can get us to do that, he knows that we will not be effective as we can be in our service to the Lord.

The remedy for his condemnation is simple. We admit that we are failures! We realize that we cannot serve God in our own strength. Indeed, we need His guidance at every moment to win victories in the spiritual realm. When we acknowledge this fact we will not fall into the condemnation of the devil.

Furthermore, the Bible tells us that we should not be condemning ourselves. Paul made this statement to the Romans.

> Therefore, there is now no condemnation for those who are in Christ Jesus (Romans 8:1 NIV).

Believers in Jesus Christ should not live their lives under any cloud of condemnation or guilt! Christ has taken all condemnation away by his death on the cross. We are still sinners, we still fail, but we have been forgiven. This is the wonderful message of the gospel. There is no condemnation for us. None!

These are some of the things which Scripture says about this evil being. It is important that we understand who he is, as well as how he operates. In this way, we can be on guard against him and his evil ways.

SUMMARY TO QUESTION 7
HOW IS SATAN'S CHARACTER DESCRIBED?

As we examine the characteristics that the Bible attributes to the devil, we obtain much insight into his evil character.

He is described as both fierce and cruel. His ferocity is compared to that of a lion. What is interesting is that both Satan and Jesus are compared to a lion. Satan is compared to a lion in the sense that he is violent and brutal while Jesus is a compared to a lion as the King over the beasts.

Satan is also described as powerful. Indeed, he is not a personage to be trifled with or taken lightly. He does have power and that power should be respected.

From the Bible we also find that Satan is a deceiver; a very cunning deceiver. He does not tell the truth.

We are also informed that he condemns believers. His methods are used to keep believers from serving Christ in the manner in which we are supposed to. He reminds each of us of our many failures.

These descriptions of the character of Satan give us further understanding of whom we are dealing with. His characteristics or attributes are not those which a Christian should imitate. Indeed, our actions should be directly the opposite of his.

What Does Satan Look Like?

Do we know what Satan looks like? Is there some way we can identify him by his appearance? What does the Bible have to say about the way the devil looks?

1. HE HAS NO HORNS, RED SUIT, OR PITCHFORK

During the Middle Ages, people would put on plays where biblical characters were portrayed. When the character of Satan came on stage, he was portrayed as an ugly individual with a red outfit, a tail, horns, and holding a pitchfork.

Today, most people immediately think of this description when someone speaks about the devil. However, this is not how the Bible describes this personage.

2. HE HAS NO PHYSICAL FORM LIKE OURS

To begin with, because Satan is a spirit-being, he has no physical form as we humans have. The Bible makes it clear that angels, who are one type of the various spirit-beings which the Lord has created, do not have any physical substance, at least not the same as humans have. The writer to the Hebrews described them in this manner.

> Are they not all ministering spirits sent forth to minister for those who will inherit salvation? (Hebrews 1:14 NKJV).

Though evil angels do not minister to God's people, they still are spirits. They do not seem to have any physical form; certainly they have no form like ours.

Satan, while some higher type of created spirit being, like the angels, would not have any physical form either.

3. HE IS AN ANGEL OF LIGHT

When he does appear, the devil appears as an angel, or "messenger," of light. This means he looks like a beautiful personage. The Apostle Paul gave the following warning about Satan.

> And it is no wonder. Even Satan tries to make himself look like an angel of light (2 Corinthians 11:14 CEV).

Because Satan is the master deceiver, coming as an angel of light, he appears as a beautiful, tempting, creature. In other words, he is not something ugly or repulsive. In fact, he looks completely opposite of what most people believe that he looks like.

Therefore, when Satan does appear in some type of visible form, he does not look like anyone would expect him to look. Consequently we could never identify him by his looks, for his appearance is meant to deceive us.

WE SHOULD BE CAREFUL OF OUTWARD APPEARANCES

We have an important illustration of this from the Old Testament. When Samuel the prophet was looking for the first rightful king of Israel, the Lord told him to look beyond the exterior. We read the following words from Him.

> But the Lord said to Samuel, "Do not look at his appearance or his stature, because I have rejected him. Man does not see what the Lord sees, for man sees what is visible, but the Lord sees the heart" (1 Samuel 16:7 HCSB).

In sum, the outward appearance is never the determining factor as to whether some thing, or some one, is from God. Indeed, we are warned that the devil comes as an angel of light. This is also true of his messengers, for they too attempt to deceive us in this manner.

The simple truth is this: be careful of outward appearances!

SUMMARY TO QUESTION 8
WHAT DOES SATAN LOOK LIKE?

When people think of Satan they usually picture an ugly looking creature wearing a red suit, with horns, while holding a pitchfork. Yet this is not how the Bible describes him. In fact, it is just the opposite.

Satan is a spirit-being, he has no physical form like humans. However, when he does appear, he does not look like the traditional picture of the devil. Indeed, the Bible says he appears as an "angel of light." In other words, he is a beautiful creature, not someone ugly or deformed looking.

Consequently, one of the tricks of the devil is to get people to associate him with ugliness. This allows him to deceive them when he appears as a thing of beauty.

The lesson for us is clear: while something may look beautiful or desirable to us this does not necessarily make it so. We can be fooled into thinking that if something appears beautiful, then it must be something good. Therefore, the outward appearance is never to be the determining factor.

As the Lord told the prophet Samuel so long ago, "People look at the outward appearance but God looks at the heart." We should certainly follow that advice.

How Does Satan Counterfeit Jesus?

The Bible says that Satan is the great counterfeiter of Jesus. We find that he has done this in a number of ways. They can be listed as follows.

1. JESUS IS THE UNIQUE SON, THE MAN OF SIN IS THE SON OF DESTRUCTION

The Lord Jesus is the unique Son of God. Indeed, He is the "One and only." We read the following description in the gospel of John.

> No one has ever seen God. The One and Only Son the One who is at the Father's side He has revealed Him (John 1:18 HCSB).

The message of the New Testament is that God the Son, the Second Person of the Holy Trinity, became a human being.

While God the Son came into our world, in a sense, Satan has his own "son," the man of sin. In fact, this person is called "the son of destruction."

> Let no one deceive you in any way. For that day will not come, unless the rebellion comes first, and the man of lawlessness is revealed, the son of destruction, who opposes and exalts himself against every so- called god or object of worship, so that he takes his seat in the temple of God, proclaiming himself to be God (2 Thessalonians 2:3,4 ESV).

Though he is not a literal offspring of Satan, this man of sin is the counterfeit of the Lord Jesus.

2. THE TRINITY AND THE UNHOLY TRINITY

The Scripture reveals that the God of the Bible is a Trinity, a tri-unity. He is made up of God the Father, God the Son, and God the Holy Spirit. While there is only one God, there are three distinct persons, or "centers of consciousness" in the one God.

Satan, in his counterfeiting of the Lord, has his own unholy trinity. This consists of himself, the beast, and the false prophet.

We read about their collective punishment in the Book of Revelation. It says.

> The Devil who deceived them was thrown into the lake of fire and sulfur where the beast and the false prophet are, and they will be tormented day and night forever and ever (Revelation 20:10 HCSB).

This seems to be a satanic counterfeit of the Holy Trinity. While the Holy Trinity will spend a glorious eternity with the believers, these three evil beings will spend their eternity in outer darkness where they will be endlessly punished for their evil.

3. EACH HAVE THEIR CHILDREN

God has His own children. They consist of those who have put their trust in Him. We read about this in the opening chapter of John's gospel. It says.

> But to all who did receive him, who believed in his name, he gave the right to become children of God (John 1:12 ESV).

Those who believe in Jesus Christ are children of God.

Satan has his own brand of children, it consists of those that practice evil. Jesus illustrated this in one of His parables where He said.

> The One who sows the good seed is the Son of Man; the field is the world; and the good seed—these are the sons of the kingdom. The weeds are the sons of the evil one (Matthew 13:37,38 HCSB).

Christ called them, "the sons of the evil one." This is another way in which the devil counterfeits the work of the Lord. He has his own people.

4. THERE ARE APOSTLES OF CHRIST AND APOSTLES OF SATAN

Jesus chose a select group of men to do His work. The Bible explains it this way.

> In these days he went out to the mountain to pray, and all night he continued in prayer to God. And when day came, he called his disciples and chose from them twelve, whom he named apostles: Simon, whom he named Peter, and Andrew his brother, and James and John, and Philip, and Bartholomew, and Matthew, and Thomas, and James the son of Alphaeus, and Simon who was called the Zealot, and Judas the son of James, and Judas Iscariot, who became a traitor (Luke 6:12-16 ESV).

After spending the night in prayer, Jesus chose His own apostles who would do His work. The Bible says they were given special authority by Him.

> These twelve Jesus sent out, instructing them, "Go nowhere among the Gentiles and enter no town of the Samaritans, but go rather to the lost sheep of the house of Israel. And proclaim as you go, saying, 'The kingdom of heaven is at hand.' Heal the sick, raise the dead, cleanse lepers, cast out demons" (Matthew 10:5-8 ESV).

We find that Satan also has his own select group of followers, his counterfeit apostles. Paul wrote to the Corinthians.

> For such people are false apostles, deceitful workers, disguising themselves as apostles of Christ (2 Corinthians 11:13 HCSB).

Like the Lord, Satan has his own apostles. These false apostles, and like their master, they are deceivers.

5. EACH MARK THOSE WHO BELONG TO THEM

God will demonstrate His seal of ownership on His servants with a mark on their forehead. The Bible records an angel saying the following words.

> Don't harm the earth or the sea or the trees until we seal the slaves of our God on their foreheads (Revelation 7:3 HCSB).

In this instance, the Lord's people have their mark, His seal of ownership.

In the same manner, Satan will have a mark of ownership placed upon his followers. We also read about this in the Book of Revelation. It says.

> He causes all, both small and great, rich and poor, free and slave, to receive a mark on their right hand or on their foreheads (Revelation 13:16 NKJV).

This is another example of Satan doing what the Lord does. Indeed, he attempts to put a mark of ownership on those whom he thinks are his.

Consequently, we find a number of ways in which Satan counterfeits the Lord.

SUMMARY TO QUESTION 9
HOW DOES SATAN COUNTERFEIT JESUS?

Satan, the great counterfeiter, has attempted to imitate and pervert the Person and character of Jesus Christ. He has done this in a number of ways. They include the following.

For one thing, he has counterfeited the unique Father-Son relationship that God the Father has with God the Son. While Jesus is the unique, one of-a-kind, Son of God, Satan will have his own son, the son of destruction. This son, while not the actual offspring of Satan, will be a human being who does his bidding by deceiving the entire world.

Satan has also counterfeited the Holy Trinity; God the Father, God the Son, and God the Holy Spirit. He has done this by means of himself and two human followers, the beast and the false prophet.

As God has His children whom He calls His own, we also find people who are called children of the devil. While God children are called the "children of light" those which belong to the devil are the "children of darkness."

Again, we have a counterfeit of those who follow the true God. Jesus Christ had His own apostles, those whom He sent to the world to represent Himself and His mission. In the same way, Satan has his apostles who represent him and his evil ways.

Finally, we are told that as the Lord puts a mark of ownership on His own people. In the same manner, the devil will do likewise. Indeed, he will insist that all people of the world have the mark of the beast which ultimately represents allegiance to him.

These are some of the ways in which this evil being has counterfeited God the Son. It is important that we are aware of these perversions.

What Contrasts Are There Between The Devil And The Holy Spirit?

The Bible makes a number of contrasts between the devil and the Person and work of God the Holy Spirit. They include the following.

1. THE SNAKE AND THE DOVE

The Holy Spirit, as well as the devil, have each appeared in animal forms. Satan comes in the form of a serpent, while the Holy Spirit has come in the form of a dove.

When Jesus was baptized, the Holy Spirit descended upon Him in bodily form, like a dove. Luke writes.

> And the Holy Spirit descended on him in the form of a dove. And a voice from heaven said, "You are my beloved Son, and I am fully pleased with you" (Luke 3:22 NLT).

While the Holy Spirit has no physical form, on this occasion, He symbolically came down upon Jesus, as the Lord was being baptized.

Satan, on the other hand, has come in the form of a snake. We read this in the Book of Revelation. It says.

> A war broke out in heaven. Michael and his angels were fighting against the dragon and its angels. But the dragon lost the battle. It and its angels were forced out of their places

in heaven and were thrown down to the earth. Yes, that old snake and his angels were thrown out of heaven! That snake, who fools everyone on earth, is known as the devil and Satan (Revelation 12:7-9 CEV).

There is the contrast between these two types of living creatures. A dove is harmless and gentile while a snake is frightful and fierce.

2. THE FATHER OF LIES AND THE SPIRIT OF TRUTH

Jesus called Satan the father of lies, while the Holy Spirit is the Spirit of truth. John recorded Jesus saying the following to the religious leaders of His day.

> Your father is the devil, and you do exactly what he wants. He has always been a murderer and a liar. There is nothing truthful about him. He speaks on his own, and everything he says is a lie. Not only is he a liar himself, but he is also the father of all lies (John 8:44 CEV).

Satan is a liar and the originator of all lies.

On the other hand, the Holy Spirit speaks the truth. Indeed, He is the Spirit of truth. Jesus said the following about Him.

> The Spirit shows what is true and will come and guide you into the full truth. The Spirit doesn't speak on his own. He will tell you only what he has heard from me, and he will let you know what is going to happen (John 16:13 CEV).

There is a complete contrast between the lying of Satan and the truth-telling of God the Holy Spirit. In fact, the contrast could not be greater.

3. A MUTE SPIRIT OR A MOUTH TO PRAISE GOD

When Satan possesses a human being through his demons, they are able to keep that person silent. The Bible describes one demon-possessed man in this manner.

After they had gone away, a demoniac who was mute was brought to him (Matthew 9:32 NRSV).

The Lord showed his authority over the devil by healing this man as well as casting out the demon.

And when the demon had been cast out, the mute man spoke. And the crowds marveled, saying, "Never was anything like this seen in Israel." But the Pharisees said, "He casts out demons by the prince of demons" (Matthew 12:33-34 ESV).

While Satan is able to keep people silent, the Holy Spirit, on the other hand, loosens the tongue of the believer to praise God. Paul wrote the following to the Ephesians.

And do not get drunk with wine, for that is debauchery, but be filled with the Spirit, addressing one another in psalms and hymns and spiritual songs, singing and making melody to the Lord with your heart (Ephesians 5:18,19 ESV).

The tongue can be used to praise or curse God. When we are controlled by the Holy Spirit our tongue praises the Lord.

4. A MURDERER OR A LIFE-GIVING SPIRIT

Satan was a murderer from the beginning. Jesus explained him in this manner.

You people are from your father the devil, and you want to do what your father desires. He was a murderer from the beginning, and does not uphold the truth, because there is no truth in him. Whenever he lies, he speaks according to his own nature, because he is a liar and the father of lies (John 8:44 NET).

Death and destruction follow Satan because he is a murderer.

75

The Holy Spirit is the one who gives life. Paul wrote the following to the Romans.

The Spirit of God, who raised Jesus from the dead, lives in you. And just as he raised Christ from the dead, he will give life to your mortal body by this same Spirit living within you (Romans 8:11 NLT).

Satan brings death, the Holy Spirit brings life.

5. THE SLANDERER AND THE ADVOCATE

The devil is a slanderer; he is one who makes accusations against believers. We read the following in the Book of Revelation.

Then I heard a loud voice in heaven say: "Now have come the salvation and the power and the kingdom of our God, and the authority of his Christ. For the accuser of our brothers, who accuses them before our God day and night, has been hurled down" (Revelation 12:10 NIV).

He slanders the people of God. Indeed, he is their accuser.

On the other hand, the Holy Spirit is the Advocate for the believer. Jesus described His mission in this manner.

And I will ask the Father, and he will give you another Advocate, to be with you forever (John 14:16 NRSV).

The Holy Spirit works on behalf of the believer while the devil works against them.

6. HE SEARCHES THE DEEP THINGS OR DEEP SECRETS

The Holy Spirit searches the "deep things" or "deep secrets" of God. Paul wrote to the Corinthians about this truth.

But we know these things because God has revealed them to us by his Spirit, and his Spirit searches out everything and shows us even God's deep secrets (1 Corinthians 2:10 NLT).

It is God's Spirit which shows us these "deep things."

Satan also has his "deep things" or "deep secrets." In the Book of Revelation we receive the following warning.

Now I say to the rest of you in Thyatira, to you who do not hold to her teaching and have not learned Satan's so-called deep secrets (I will not impose any other burden on you) (Revelation 2:24 NIV).

While it is the job of the Holy Spirit to search out the deep things of God we find that Satan, too, has his deep things, his deep secrets.

In sum, there are a number of contrasts between this personage the devil and the Third Person of the Trinity, God the Holy Spirit. As we can see, their character could not be more different.

SUMMARY TO QUESTION 10
WHAT CONTRASTS ARE THERE BETWEEN THE DEVIL AND THE HOLY SPIRIT?

Interestingly, we find that there are a number of contrasts that the Bible gives between Satan and the Holy Spirit; the Third Person of the Trinity. We can summarize them in the following manner.

Each is described in Scripture as coming in the form of a living creature to people here upon the earth. While Satan is the snake, the Holy Spirit is the dove. The comparisons are obvious. The dove is harmless while the snake is deadly.

Furthermore, we have the comparison in the manner of truth. The Holy Spirit is the Spirit of truth, while Satan is a liar, and the Father of lies. Again, their character is the complete opposite of one another.

The Bible says that when Satan possesses someone he has the ability to make them mute. When the Holy Spirit controls a person their tongue is used to praise the living God.

Scripture also says that the Holy Spirit is a life-giving Spirit. Indeed, He gives spiritual life to the believer. On the other hand, Satan is a murderer. The contrast could not be greater.

In another contrast we are told that Satan is the slanderer of God's people, while the Holy Spirit is the Advocate of the believer. Satan attempts to pull Christians down while the Holy Spirit builds us up.

Finally, the Holy Spirit searches the deep things of God, He teaches believers God's truth. In contrast, we are told Satan also has his deep things also. There is a depth to his evil.

These are some of the many contrasts Scripture gives us between God the Holy Spirit and Satan. As we can readily observe, their characteristics could not be more different.

Does Satan Have
His Own Kingdom?

Does Satan have his own kingdom? Does he have his own subjects? What does the Bible say about this issue?

THE OFFER OF SATAN TO JESUS

When tempting Jesus, we find that the devil offered Him a kingdom. Matthew recorded what took place as follows.

> And the devil took him up and showed him all the king-doms of the world in a moment of time, and said to him, "To you I will give all this authority and their glory, for it has been delivered to me, and I give it to whom I will" (Luke 4:5,6 ESV).

Was Satan correct in saying that the kingdoms of the world system are under his authority? Were they his to give?

There is a difference of opinion among Christians as to whether Satan has his own kingdom today. We can summarize the options in the following manner.

OPTION 1: SATAN HAS NO KINGDOM

There are those who say that Satan has no kingdom whatsoever today. He was totally defeated by Jesus Christ at Calvary's cross, and is now bound in the bottomless pit. The offer he made to Jesus at the temptation was something which he was not in a position to make. The kingdoms were never his to give.

OPTION 2: SATAN PRESENTLY HAS A KINGDOM

Other Bible believers hold that Satan has a powerful kingdom. He is the leader of a vast army of evil spirits that are constantly at work today. Though some angels are bound, others are not. Unbelievers are said to be under the authority of Satan and his power. The Bible says the purpose of Jesus' coming was to do the following.

> To open their eyes so they may turn from darkness to light, and from the power of Satan to God. Then they will receive forgiveness for their sins and be given a place among God's people, who are set apart by faith in me (Acts 26:18 NLT).

Unbelievers are still, in some sense, under the authority of Satan.

THE EVIDENCE FOR SATAN'S KINGDOM

The fact that Satan has some sort of kingdom can be seen in a statement of Jesus. He said the following to the religious leaders of His day.

> Jesus knew their thoughts and replied, "Any kingdom at war with itself is doomed. A city or home divided against itself is doomed. And if Satan is casting out Satan, he is fighting against himself. His own kingdom will not survive" (Matthew 12:25,26 NLT).

Jesus told them that it would not make sense to argue that Satan is fighting against Satan. Otherwise his kingdom would fail. This statement of the Lord seems to assume that the devil has some type of kingdom.

Furthermore, even after the death and resurrection of Christ, the Bible says that Satan is the god of this word, the ruler of the authority of the air. Paul wrote.

> In their case the god of this world has blinded the minds
> of the unbelievers, to keep them from seeing the light of
> the gospel of the glory of Christ, who is the image of God
> (2 Corinthians 4:4 ESV).

He is called the "god of this world," or the "god of this age."

In another place, Paul wrote that Satan has authority over this world-system. We read the following in his letter to the Ephesians.

> You used to live just like the rest of the world, full of sin,
> obeying Satan, the mighty prince of the power of the air. He
> is the spirit at work in the hearts of those who refuse to obey
> God (Ephesians 2:2 NLT).

While Satan may have a kingdom, it is at best only temporary.

SATAN HAS BEEN DEFEATED

All believers agree that Satan has been defeated by Jesus Christ. Indeed, on the night of His betrayal Jesus Himself said.

> Now is the time for judgment on this world; now the prince
> of this world will be driven out (John 12:31 NIV).

The ruler of this world has been driven out. He has been defeated!

Earlier, during Jesus' public ministry, He sent out seventy-two disciples to preach His message throughout Israel. In addition, to preaching the message, they were given power over the demonic realm. The Bible records the response of these disciples when they returned to Jesus.

> The seventy-two returned with joy and said, "Lord, even the
> demons submit to us in your name." He replied, "I saw Satan
> fall like lightning from heaven" (Luke 10:17,18 NIV).

Satan and his demonic forces were defeated by Jesus' disciples; the ones who were sent out in His power.

81

JESUS TRIUMPHED OVER SATAN

Consequently, the good news is that Jesus has indeed triumphed over Satan. The Apostle Paul wrote about this triumph of Jesus.

> God wiped out the charges that were against us for disobeying the Law of Moses. He took them away and nailed them to the cross. There Christ defeated all powers and forces. He let the whole world see them being led away as prisoners when he celebrated his victory (Colossians 2:14,15 CEV).

Satan and his forces have been defeated.

The real issue is, "In what sense has he been defeated?" Has his defeat at the cross caused him to be permanently bound in the bottomless pit, or is that binding of Satan something yet future? Will it happen only when Jesus Christ returns a second time?

In sum, the Bible seems to teach that the binding of Satan is still yet future.

Therefore, the final results of this defeat will be seen only at the time Christ returns. Until then, Satan is working his evil in the world.

SUMMARY TO QUESTION 11
DOES SATAN HAVE HIS OWN KINGDOM?

In the New Testament we are told that Satan offered Jesus Christ the kingdoms of this world because he claimed to have authority over them. There is no question that the devil offered these kingdoms to Jesus.

However, there is a question as to whether the claim of Satan was legitimate. Indeed, this issue has divided believers. Could he truly offer the kingdoms of this world to Christ? Does Satan presently have some sort of a kingdom?

There are those who say that Satan has been totally defeated by Jesus Christ on the cross, and, therefore, he has no kingdom as of now. Whether or not he had a kingdom at the time of Jesus' temptation is a non-issue.

Today, he has been defeated and judged and thus he rules no kingdom whatsoever. Indeed, he is presently bound in the abyss, the bottomless pit.

Others, while acknowledging Satan's defeat on the cross, do not believe his punishment will be fully realized until Jesus Christ returns. During this interval period, Satan is ruling this evil world system as the god of this age, the ruler over the authority of the air. Therefore, this world, in some sense, is still his kingdom.

Consequently, he ruled a kingdom at the time he offered it to Jesus, and in some sense he still has this evil kingdom. When Christ returns, however, his rule and reign over this world will end.

QUESTION 12

Did God Create
The Devil?

No. Though it is commonly believed that God created the devil this is a misconception about what occurred. Indeed, nowhere in the Bible are we told that it was God who created this personage as evil. The Bible says the following about what God created.

1. GOD CREATED ALL THINGS

God is the Creator of all things. This is the clear teaching of Scripture. Paul wrote the following to the Ephesians.

> And to make all see what *is* the fellowship of the mystery, which from the beginning of the ages has been hidden in God who created all things through Jesus Christ (Ephesians 3:9 NKJV).

Notice Paul said that God has created "all things."

Indeed, God is said to have created the heaven and the earth. The familiar first verse of the Bible reads as follows.

> In the beginning God created the heaven and the earth (Genesis 1:1 KJV).

No doubt, God is the Creator of everything.

2. HE MADE EVERYTHING VERY GOOD

In addition, the Bible says that God created all things "very good." We read of this in the first chapter of Genesis. It says.

> God looked at what he had done. All of it was very good!
> Evening came and then morning—that was the sixth day
> (Genesis 1:31 CEV).

"Everything" would include the angels, as well as the other spirit-beings, the cherubim, seraphim, and living creatures, that God created.

3. THERE WAS ONLY ONE WILL IN THE UNIVERSE

At this time, there was only one will in the universe, the will of God. We read the following in the Book of Revelation.

> You are worthy, O Lord, To receive glory and honor and
> power; For You created all things, And by Your will they exist
> and were created (Revelation 4:11 NKJV).

Every creature was in obedience with that one will. Perfection was everywhere. There was no such thing as sin or evil in the universe.

4. ONE CREATED BEING CHOSE TO REBEL

Though everything in God's creation was perfect, angels, as well as the other spirit-beings God created, like humans, were created with choice. In other words, they were not made as robots. The Bible seems to teach that one of these spirit-beings, at some point in time, decided to rebel against God.

5. HIS EXERCISED HIS OWN WILL

This creature decided to bring his own will into the universe. Instead of following the Lord, this personage went off in his own direction. In the Book of Isaiah, we seemingly have a description of this rebellion. He wrote the following.

You said in your heart, "I will ascend to heaven; I will raise my throne above the stars of God; I will sit on the mount of assembly on the heights of Zaphon; I will ascend to the tops of the clouds, I will make myself like the Most High" (Isaiah 14:13,14 NRSV).

This creature decided to bring his own will into the universe, a will that was contrary to what God wanted.

6. HE BECAME SATAN

When this act of rebellion occurred, this spirit-being became Satan, or " adversary." Therefore, a new type of being came into existence, one in which God did not create. Indeed, there was now a sinful being. This came as a result of his choice, not because of God's original design or intent.

The Bible speaks of the angels that sinned.

For if God did not spare the angels who sinned, but threw them into hell and locked them up in chains in utter darkness, to be kept until the judgment (2 Peter 2:4 NET).

Satan was either one of those angels which sinned, or more likely, a higher type of created being. He is the personage who led these angels to follow him and abandon the Lord.

7. THIS WAS THE ORIGINATION OF SIN

The Bible says that Satan was the originator of sin. In fact, Jesus said that he sinned from the beginning. John records Jesus saying.

You are from your father the devil, and you choose to do your father's desires. He was a murderer from the beginning and does not stand in the truth, because there is no truth in him. When he lies, he speaks according to his own nature, for he is a liar and the father of lies (John 8:44 NRSV).

Jesus described him as a liar from the beginning, as well as a murderer.

The Apostle John described him as one who had sinned from the beginning. We read.

> Anyone who keeps on sinning belongs to the devil. He has sinned from the beginning, but the Son of God came to destroy all that he has done (1 John 3:8 CEV).

Such is the inglorious beginning of this spirit-being who became the devil.

In sum, we can say that God did not create the devil but rather created all of the angels, as well as other spirit-beings, with choice. One of these personages led a rebellion which caused sin to enter. He then became the devil, the adversary. This seems to be the best way in which to understand what Scripture has to say about the topic.

SUMMARY TO QUESTION 12
DID GOD CREATE THE DEVIL?

While it is commonly believed that the devil, Satan, is actually a creation of God, the Bible does not teach this. While the devil is a real personage the Bible says that God did not create him! A number of important points need to be made along this line.

Scripture makes it clear that everything that God created in the universe was originally perfect. This includes all created beings, the angels, as well as other spirit beings like the cherubim, living creatures, and the seraphim.

Though every creature was originally created perfect, each one was given the power of choice. In other words, obedience to the Lord was ultimately up to them. They could choose to obey the Lord or disobey Him.

One particular spirit-being did choose to rebel against God. It seems that he tried to impose his own will, rather than following God's will.

He also convinced other spirit beings, angels, to rebel with him. When this rebellion occurred, this personage became the adversary of God, Satan. Indeed, the word "Satan" means, "the adversary."

Therefore, this particular creature was not created to be God's adversary but rather he became the devil through his disobedient behavior.

In sum, he was given choice and with that choice this being decided to rebel against the Lord.

Therefore, God did not create this creature in this manner, nor did He wish him to rebel. It was the choice of this personage that he would become the devil. Consequently, God did not create the devil.

QUESTION 13

What Caused
Satan's Fall?

The Bible says that when a mighty created being rebelled against God, he became the devil. Scripture gives us some insight as to what it was that caused the fall of this personage. The Bible says the following.

1. PRIDE

As we examine the Bible, we find that pride was a factor in Satan's fall. In a passage that may speak of the original fall of this specially created being, we read the following description.

> Your heart was proud because of your beauty; you corrupted your wisdom for the sake of your splendor. I cast you to the ground; I exposed you before kings, to feast their eyes on you (Ezekiel 28:17 ESV).

In this verse, pride in his own beauty was the sin that caused this personage to be corrupt.

The New Testament also connects the sin of pride with the devil. Paul wrote the following words to Timothy.

> He must not be a recent convert, or he may be puffed up with conceit and fall into the condemnation of the devil (1 Timothy 3:6 NRSV).

Pride and conceit is associated to the devil.

We also find that pride is at the top of the list of sins that God hates. Indeed, in the Book of Proverbs, we read the following list of sins.

> There are six things the LORD hates—no, seven things he detests: haughty eyes, a lying tongue, hands that kill the innocent (Proverbs 6:16,17 NLT).

"Haughty eyes," or pride, is at the top of the list of the things which the Lord hates. Realizing this should certainly cause us to avoid being proud.

In addition, the Bible warns us as to what pride will lead to.

> Pride goes before destruction, a haughty spirit before a fall (Proverbs 16:18 NIV).

The fact that God hates prides testifies to horrific nature of the sin of this personage who became the devil

2. HE HAD SELFISH AMBITION

A second cause for the fall of Satan was selfish ambition. In other words, this personage wanted to be somebody that he was not.

In another passage, that appears to give us insight into his fall from his lofty status, we read the following.

> How you have fallen from heaven, morning star, son of the dawn! You have been cast down to the earth, you who once laid low the nations! You said in your heart, "I will ascend to the heavens; I will raise my throne above the stars of God; I will sit enthroned on the mount of assembly, on the utmost heights of Mount Zaphon. I will ascend above the tops of the clouds; I will make myself like the Most High" (Isaiah 14:12-14 NIV).

The selfish ambition of this created being caused him to lead a rebellion against God. This rebellion continues to this day. It will only come to an end when he is thrown into the lake of fire.

In sum, it seems that it was pride, as well as selfish ambition, which caused the downfall of this personage who became the devil.

SUMMARY TO QUESTION 13
WHAT CAUSED SATAN'S FALL?

The Bible never specifically speaks of the fall of the created being who became Satan, the adversary of God. However, it seems possible to derive some information about his fall from several passages in Scripture. From what is written, it seems that the fall of this personage who became the devil was rooted in two basic sins; pride and selfish ambition.

We are told that this personage, who was a beautiful creature, was lifted up with pride. His pride caused him to want something that was not rightfully his, the same adoration as God.

This sin is all the more awful when we discover that pride is at the top of the list of things which God hates. Indeed, the Bible warns that pride goes before a fall. Therefore, those of us who want to please God should be careful not to be lifted up with pride as we seek to serve Him.

Not only was this beautiful created personage proud, he wanted to be something which he was not. Selfish ambition led him to rebel against the God of the Bible. Certain, angels, who are other supernaturally created beings, then joined him in his revolt against the Lord.

Consequently, these sins caused his downfall, as well as the downfall of those angels who went with him. It has also been the downfall of many people since that time.

Pride and selfish ambition, the sins of the devil, are sins which we should take pains to avoid.

What Were The Results
Of Satan's Fall?

The fall of Satan, the created being who became the devil, the "adversary," resulted in a number of things. They include the following.

1. HE BECAME THE FIRST SINNER IN THE UNIVERSE

When this created being rebelled against God, His Creator, and became the devil, he became the first sinner in the universe. Scripture emphasizes that he sinned in the very beginning. In his first letter to the believers, John wrote the following.

> Anyone who keeps on sinning belongs to the devil. He has sinned from the beginning, but the Son of God came to destroy all that he has done (1 John 3:8 CEV).

The particular being who rebelled against God in the beginning had the dubious distinction of becoming the first sinner in the universe.

2. SATAN BECAME THE AUTHOR OF SIN

Because he was the first sinner, he is the author of, and basis for, all subsequent sin. Jesus said to the religious rulers of His day.

> You are from your father the devil, and you choose to do your father's desires. He was a murderer from the beginning and does not stand in the truth, because there is no truth in

him. When he lies, he speaks according to his own nature, for he is a liar and the father of lies (John 8:44 NRSV).

This particular being became the author of sin.

3. HIS GREAT WISDOM WAS MADE CORRUPT THROUGH SIN

Though this personage had great knowledge and wisdom, it was now corrupted through his sin. We read the following in Ezekiel.

Your heart became proud because of your beauty; For the sake of your splendor you corrupted your wisdom. So I threw you down to the earth; I made you a spectacle before kings (Ezekiel 28:17 HCSB).

Sin brought corruption to his wisdom.

4. HE WAS COMPLETELY TAKEN OVER BY SIN

The fall of Satan was complete to the extent that he was totally taken over by sin. As Jesus told the religious leaders of His day, "He is the father of lies." The Lord said of them.

You are from your father the devil. When he lies, he speaks according to his own nature, for he is a liar and the father of lies (John 8:44 NRSV).

Sin completely took over this personage to the extent that he was the first liar and the originator of all lies.

5. HIS SIN CAUSED HIM TO BE CONDEMNED

Because of his sin, this specially created being has fallen under God's condemnation. The Bible records the following judgment he will receive.

How you are fallen from heaven, O Day Star, son of Dawn! How you are cut down to the ground, you who laid the nations low! (Isaiah 14:12 NRSV).

This created being, though beautiful and intelligent, will be cut down to the ground. Though under God's judgment, he still has some access to God. We read in the Book of Job.

> Now there was a day when the sons of God came to present themselves before the LORD, and Satan came also among them (Job 1:6 KJV).

While this passage tells us that the devil can still come into God's presence, it does not tell us anything further about the access which he is granted.

6. HE WILL BE SENT DOWN TO THE EARTH

Eventually Satan will only have access to the earth. We read about this in the Book of Revelation. It says he will be cast out of heaven.

> Now war arose in heaven, Michael and his angels fighting against the dragon. And the dragon and his angels fought back, but he was defeated, and there was no longer any place for them in heaven. And the great dragon was thrown down, that ancient serpent, who is called the devil and Satan, the deceiver of the whole world—he was thrown down to the earth, and his angels were thrown down with him (Revelation 12:7-9 ESV).

At a future time, this evil being will be limited to the earth.

7. HE WILL EVENTUALLY BE PUNISHED

The original sin of the devil will result in his ultimate destiny; eternal separation from God as well as eternal punishment. The Bible says.

> When the thousand years are over, Satan will be released from his prison and will go out to deceive the nations in the four corners of the earth—Gog and Magog—to gather them for battle. In number they are like the sand on the

seashore. They marched across the breadth of the earth and surrounded the camp of God's people, the city he loves. But fire came down from heaven and devoured them. And the devil, who deceived them, was thrown into the lake of burning sulfur, where the beast and the false prophet had been thrown. They will be tormented day and night for ever and ever (Revelation 20:7-10 NIV).

Punishment is coming for this evil personage. Indeed, he will have to pay the ultimate penalty for his sin.

In sum, we can conclude that the fall of this beautiful intelligent being who became Satan resulted in his ruin, as well as the ruin of many others.

SUMMARY TO QUESTION 14
WHAT WERE THE RESULTS OF SATAN'S FALL?

It seems from a study of the totality of Scripture that the devil, Satan, was originally a highly ranked specially created being who fell from his perfect state. If this is the case, then there were a number of results that occurred when this personage fell and became Satan, the adversary.

First, this individual had the distinction of being the first sinner in the universe. This means that he is also the author of sin. All sin can be traced back to him.

We also find that his great wisdom was corrupted through sin. While he may have been the wisest of all the created beings the Lord had made, this personage made a terrible decision by staging a rebellion against God.

There is more. This personage was completely taken over by sin. He became total sin, the embodiment of sin.

We also learn that His sin caused him to be condemned by the Lord. Judgment was pronounced upon him for his rebellion.

Eventually he will be thrown out of heaven and sent down to the earth. No longer will he have any access to the heavenly realm.

Finally, he will experience the ultimate judgment which will result in conscious punishment for all eternity. This summarizes the consequences of his rebellion.

Where Does Satan Presently Live?

There are those who believe that Satan is presently bound in the bottomless pit. The Bible does say that he will be there someday. We read the following in the Book of Revelation.

> Then I saw an angel coming down from heaven, holding in his hand the key to the bottomless pit and a great chain. He seized the dragon, that ancient serpent, who is the Devil and Satan, and bound him for a thousand years, and threw him into the pit, and locked and sealed it over him, so that he would deceive the nations no more, until the thousand years were ended. After that he must be let out for a little while (Revelation 20:1-3 NRSV).

Some Bible students think this binding of Satan happened some time in the past. They do not believe that it will take place at a future time.

1. HE IS NOT IMPRISONED IN HELL

A common belief is to think that Satan and his angels are presently imprisoned in hell. However the Bible does not teach this at all. A number of points need to be mentioned.

HE HAS ACCESS TO GOD

Satan presently has access to God. We read about this in the Book of Job where the following incident is recorded.

Now there was a day when the sons of God came to present themselves before the LORD, and Satan came also among them (Job 1:6 KJV).

This access does not seem to be anything abnormal. Therefore, it appears as though he can approach God whenever he wishes. However, since we have so little information about this, we can only suggest tentative answers.

HE LIVES IN THE HEAVENLY REALM

The abode of Satan is in the heavenly realm. Paul wrote about our struggle with evil powers when he wrote to the Ephesians. He said.

For our struggle is not against enemies of blood and flesh, but against the rulers, against the authorities, against the cosmic powers of this present darkness, against the spiritual forces of evil in the heavenly places (Ephesians 6:12 NRSV).

It is in this sphere, the unseen heavenly realm, where the devil resides.

HE IS ACTIVE UPON THE EARTH

Scripture says that Satan is also active upon the earth. The Bible says the following in the Book of Job.

The LORD said to Satan, "Where have you come from?" Satan answered the LORD, "From going to and fro on the earth, and from walking up and down on it" (Job 1:7 NRSV).

This shows that he was doing his evil work upon the earth after his original fall.

From the New Testament, we find that he is still free to do evil. In fact, we are warned that he now roams the earth like a roaring lion.

Be self-controlled and alert. Your enemy the devil prowls around like a roaring lion looking for someone to devour (1 Peter 5:8 NIV).

From all of the above, we find that Satan is not presently restricted to one place. To the contrary, he can travel to a number of places. The time when he is bound in captivity is still future.

WAS HE CAST OUT OF GOD'S PRESENCE AT HIS FALL?

The fact that Satan will eventually be thrown down to the earth brings up a question. Was this being cast out of heaven when he originally sinned against the Lord? The casting of Satan out of heaven, which is recorded in the Book of Revelation, can seemingly mean one of two things.

First, either Satan will be thrown out of God's presence only at a particular point in history, which is still future. This means he still has access to the Lord today.

The second possibility is that he had previously been thrown out of God's presence, but still had limited access to the stellar heavens, the place where God makes His presence known.

Some feel that he was cast out of God' presence the moment he sinned and now only has temporary access to the Lord. This access is alluded to in the reference in the Book of Job where Satan approaches God.

Others feel that he was not banished from God's presence when he sinned but rather will be only at this point that the Book of Revelation records (Revelation 12).

As is the case with many of these questions, there does not seem to be enough information to be certain of the answer.

Consequently, we can only offer tentative conclusions at best.

SUMMARY TO QUESTION 15
WHERE DOES SATAN PRESENTLY LIVE?

There is some question among Bible students about the present location of Satan.

The Bible speaks of a time when he will be thrown out of heaven down to the earth. He will then be bound in a bottomless pit. There are those who believe that this has already happened, while others believe this will occur in the future.

According to Scripture, at one particular time, Satan had access to the Lord. The Book of Job says that Satan could actually approach the throne of the Lord. As to whether this is still the case is a matter of debate.

Though not everyone will agree, it seems that the best answer is to assume that Satan has not yet been bound in the bottomless pit. This will occur in the future after the Second Coming of Jesus Christ.

Whether he has complete access to the Lord at this particular time, or only limited access, we are not clearly told.

Why Did God Allow
To Continue After He Rebelled?

There are several questions which are usually asked about the original rebellion of the created being who became Satan, the devil. They include the following difficult issues.

1. WHY DID GOD CREATE HIM?

First, why did God create this spirit-being if He knew that he was going to rebel? Since God does know everything, He certainly knew that this personage would eventually sin against him. Why, then, was he created in the first place?

2. WHY ALLOW HIM TO CONTINUE?

Second, why did He allow this created being to rebel? Since God created this personage, He could have kept him from rebelling against Him. Indeed, steps could have been taken to make it impossible for any type of rebellion led by this created being. Why didn't God take these steps so there would be no sin on his part, and then the rebellion of some of the angels?

3. WHY NOT DESTROY HIM IMMEDIATELY?

Finally, after this personage sinned, and became Satan, the adversary, why didn't God immediately destroy him? So much pain and suffering could have been avoided if his original sin had been immediately punished. Why didn't God do it?

4. NO ANSWERS ARE GIVEN TO THESE QUESTIONS

The Bible does not give us any specific answers to these "why" questions. Part of the reason, as to why these questions have no answers, has to do with the nature of the Bible. Scripture is God's revelation about His dealings with humanity. This is the main story. The work of Satan, and his angels, are only incidental to the message of Scripture.

Consequently, much about him, and his deeds, are not explained. Neither does God explain these "why" questions with respect to him.

Though the Bible does not give us any specific answers to these "why" questions about Satan, this has not kept people from speculating. The problem with this type of speculation is that no one is able to know the right answer. For whatever reason, God has not told us "why." We should leave it at that.

WHAT WE DO KNOW FOR CERTAIN

Rather than speculating about what we do not know, we should concentrate on what we do know. We can sum them up as follows.

1. GOD KNOWS ALL THINGS

God certainly did know all these things would happen. He is all-knowing. In other words, nothing escapes His notice. Jesus said the following about God the Father.

> Aren't two sparrows sold for only a penny? But your Father knows when any one of them falls to the ground. Even the hairs on your head are counted (Matthew 10:29,30 CEV).

The Bible is clear that God know all things. Indeed, His knowledge is exhaustive.

2. HE HAS NOT TOLD US EVERYTHING

The Bible also says that God has not told us everything about Himself, or His plan. In the Book of Deuteronomy, we find the following statement about the Lord.

There are secret things that belong to the LORD our God, but the revealed things belong to us and our descendants forever, so that we may obey these words of the law (Deuteronomy 29:29 NLT).

There are many things in heaven and on earth that the Lord does not reveal to us. This is something which we must always appreciate.

3. HIS WAYS ARE NOT OUR WAYS

The Bible makes it clear that God's ways are beyond our ways. Isaiah the prophet records the Lord saying the following.

"For My thoughts are not your thoughts, and your ways are not My ways." This is the Lord's declaration. "For as heaven is higher than earth, so My ways are higher than your ways, and My thoughts than your thoughts" (Isaiah 55:8,9 HCSB).

This is something we must always remember. God works in ways that are higher than our ways and His thoughts are higher than our thoughts.

Because His ways are not our ways, they are past our finding out, we cannot discover them. Paul wrote to the Romans.

Who can measure the wealth and wisdom and knowledge of God? Who can understand his decisions or explain what he does? (Romans 11:33 CEV).

We, as limited human beings, cannot discover how the Lord works. He is all-knowing while we certainly are not. Indeed, we cannot understand or explain what He does.

Therefore, many of our "why" questions will remain unanswered.

SUMMARY TO QUESTION 16
WHY DID GOD ALLOW SATAN TO CONTINUE AFTER HE REBELLED?

There are several questions about the origin, fall, and continued existence of the devil that we all would like to understand. Why did He create this personage who became the devil when He knew that he would eventually rebel? When he did rebel, why didn't the Lord destroy this evil creature right away? These are questions that humans have continually asked.

God has not revealed to us the answers to these questions. There seem to be a number of reasons as to why this is so. We can list them as follows.

First, the lack of an answer to these questions has to do with the main message of Scripture, God and His relationship to humanity. Since these "why" questions about the devil are not directly pertinent to the message of the Bible, God has not revealed the answers to us. In other words, we don't need to know them.

Though people have speculated as to why God allowed these things to happen, ultimately we do not know the answer. Since we don't ultimately know, we should not speculate.

However, there are several things which we do know. They include the following.

For one thing, we do know that God has all knowledge. Indeed, nothing escapes His notice.

This means that He did know that this created being would rebel, and that he would cause so much grief and suffering. Therefore, God certainly knew the consequences of this satanic rebellion.

While God knew this would happen, He still allowed these events to unfold.

Because the Lord tells us that His ways are past finding out, we should rest in the fact that God has an overall plan that took into consideration the rebellion and the sin of the devil. That should be a sufficient answer for us.

Why Is Satan Sometimes
Called Lucifer?

In some versions of the Bible, the personage described in Isaiah 14:12 is called by the name "Lucifer." For example, the King James Version reads as follows.

> How art thou fallen from heaven, O Lucifer, son of the morning! how art thou cut down to the ground, which did weaken the nations! (Isaiah 14:12 KJV).

The proper name "Lucifer" appears nowhere else in the *King James Version.*

Other versions however do not use the name Lucifer to describe this same personage in Isaiah 14:12. For example, the *American Standard Version* of 1901 reads.

> How art thou fallen from heaven, O day-star, son of the morning! how art thou cut down to the ground, that did lay low the nations! (Isaiah 14:12 ASV).

Most other modern versions translate this passage in a similar way as the American Standard Version.

WHY THE DIFFERENCE?

To understand the difference we must go back to the original language in Isaiah 14:12, Hebrew. The Hebrew word translated "day star," or

"Lucifer" is *Helel.* This word has been rendered in a number of ways, because there is some question as to its exact meaning, and how it should be understood.

We can make the following observations about this issue.

OPTION 1: THE WORD MAY MEAN "TO HOWL"

Helel has been understood to be the command form of the verb, "to howl." Therefore the translation of Isaiah 14:12 would read, "Howl, son of the morning."

OPTION 2: THE WORD MAY MEAN SHINING ONE

Others have connected this word with the verb, "to shine." From this idea came "day star," "shining one," "bearer of light," or "morning star." We will list of sampling of how some English versions translate it with this understanding of the word.

The New English translation reads as follows.

> Look how you have fallen from the sky, O shining one, son of the dawn! (Isaiah 14:12 NET).

The NET Bible has the following note to explain its translation.

The Hebrew text has (*helel ben-shakhar,* "Helel son of Shachar"), which is probably a name for the morning star (Venus) or the crescent moon (NET Bible, Note on Isaiah 14:12).

The New International Version reads.

> How you have fallen from heaven, morning star, son of the dawn (Isaiah 14:12 NIV).

The Holman Christian Standard Bible says.

> Shining morning star, how you have fallen from the heavens (Isaiah 14:12 HCSB).

The English Standard Version has the following translation.

How you are fallen from heaven, O Day Star, son of Dawn (Isaiah 14:12 ESV).

As we can observe, there are many ways it has been translated if one understands the word to mean something like "shining one."

OPTION 3: IT IS POSSIBLY A PROPER NAME

In the context of Isaiah, *Helel* is possibly used as proper name for the king of Babylon. Therefore his name would be translated as "day star," or "bright one."

THE HEBREW WAS TRANSLATED INTO LATIN AS LUCIFER

When this Hebrew term was translated into Latin, the word *lucifer* was used. The verb *lucifero* basically means "to shine." Therefore, if this term is understood to be a proper name of the King of Babylon, that name, in noun form in Latin, would be *lucifer*.

THE KING JAMES TRANSLATORS

The *King James* translators were very familiar with Latin. In fact, the notes they kept during their translation deliberations were made in Latin. When they began their translation process, the Latin Vulgate translation of the Bible had been around for a thousand years. *Lucifer*, the Latin translation of the Hebrew *Helel*, had already become a proper name for the devil.

Instead of translating the term as "day star" or "bright one," they kept the popular Latin term "lucifer." This is how the term ended up in some English translations.

JESUS IS THE BRIGHT AND MORNING STAR

Though the term "day star" has been attributed to the devil, the genuine bright "Morning Star" is Jesus Christ. We find Jesus saying the following.

I, Jesus, have sent my angel to give you this testimony for the churches. I am the Root and the Offspring of David, and the bright Morning Star (Revelation 22:16 NIV).

The genuine Morning Star is the Lord Jesus Himself, not the devil.

JESUS AS LUCIFER?

Peter uses the same term "Morning Star" to describe Jesus. He wrote.

Moreover, we possess the prophetic word as an altogether reliable thing. You do well if you pay attention to this as you would to a light shining in a murky place, until the day dawns and the morning star rises in your hearts (2 Peter 1:19 NET).

Interestingly, the Latin Vulgate translates the Greek term here for "Morning Star" as lucifer! This of course does not equate Jesus with the devil. It just goes to show how a term like "lucifer" can develop meanings in the English language that were never part of the original Greek or Hebrew.

In sum, we can conclude that the Hebrew term translated as the proper name "lucifer" in some Bible versions has a number of possible ways in which it can be understood.

SUMMARY TO QUESTION 17
WHY IS SATAN CALLED LUCIFER?

One of the popular names for the fallen being, who became the devil, is Lucifer. The reason as to why Lucifer has been understood to be a proper name of the devil has to do with the Latin translation of the Hebrew term *Helel*. This word was understood, by some, to be a proper name for the King of Babylon. It means "light bearer," or *lucifer* in Latin.

The Latin title became a popular name for this evil figure. When the King James translators rendered the Hebrew term into English, they kept the popular term "lucifer" for the devil. This simply states how this personage became known as Lucifer, or the "light bearer."

Other English translations do not view this Hebrew term as a proper name. Some render this word as a command form of the verb "howl." Others translate it as a noun such as "day star" or "shining one." There is no consensus as to how it should be translated.

What Are Some Of The Different Titles Of Satan?

Satan, the devil, has been given a number of names or titles in Scripture. While some of the names attributed to Satan may not actually be referring to him, the following names have been assumed by Bible students to be names of the devil. They are as follows.

1. SATAN

This is one of his primary names. Indeed, fifty-two times in Scripture this being is designated as Satan, or the adversary. For example, we read in Job.

> Now there was a day when the sons of God came to present themselves before the LORD, and Satan came also among them (Job 1:6 KJV).

This is the probably the name by which he is the best known.

2. DAY-STAR

In the Book of Isaiah there is a section about the King of Babylon. However, many commentators believe it is speaking about more than a mere earthly king. Indeed, they believe that it is speaking of the devil himself.

In this passage, this personage is called the "day star." This has the idea of "bearer of light." This name, translated into Latin, is "lucifer." This seems to be the name of Satan before his fall.

> How you are fallen from heaven, O Day Star, son of Dawn! How you are cut down to the ground, you who laid the nations low! (Isaiah 14:12 NRSV).

He is called the "Day Star, son of Dawn in this passage.

Yet we find that the true "Day Star" and "Bearer of Light" is the Lord Jesus Himself. We read about this at the end of the Book of Revelation where Jesus gave this testimony about His identity.

> I, Jesus, have sent my angel to testify to you about these things for the churches. I am the root and the descendant of David, the bright morning star (Revelation 22:16 ESV).

Jesus is the bright "Morning Star."

Scripture also says that Jesus is the "true light." In the introduction to his gospel, John wrote of Him in the following manner.

> The true light, which enlightens everyone, was coming into the world (John 1:9 NRSV).

This is the contrast between Satan and Jesus.

3. SON OF THE MORNING (SON OF DAWN)

He is also titled "son of the morning" or the "son of dawn."

> How you are fallen from heaven, O Day Star, son of Dawn! How you are cut down to the ground, you who laid the nations low! (Isaiah 14:12 NRSV).

The prophet Isaiah records this title which the Lord gave him.

4. THE ANOINTED CHERUB

This personage was also called the "anointed cherub." We read this description from the writings of the prophet Ezekiel.

> You were an anointed guardian cherub. I placed you; you were on the holy mountain of God; in the midst of the stones of fire you walked (Ezekiel 28:14 ESV).

Scripture speaks of several different types of created beings including cherubim, seraphim, living creatures, and angels. This title seems to place him above all the other created beings that the Lord had made.

5. THE DEVIL

Along with the title "Satan," this is the most popular name for this personage. The references to "the devil" only appear in the New Testament. For example, we read of Jesus' temptation in Matthew's gospel.

> Then was Jesus led up of the Spirit into the wilderness to be tempted of the devil (Matthew 4:1 KJV).

The devil literally means "slanderer." Satan is called this because he slanders both God and humanity.

In the Garden of Eden, we find that he slandered God's character. Scripture records the following dialogue between the snake, who represented the devil, and the woman Eve.

> The woman said to the serpent, "We may eat fruit from the trees in the garden, but God did say, 'You must not eat fruit from the tree that is in the middle of the garden, and you must not touch it, or you will die.'" "You will not surely die," the serpent said to the woman. "For God knows that when you eat of it your eyes will be opened, and you will be like God, knowing good and evil" (Genesis 3:2-5 NIV).

Note that he accused the Lord God of holding back good things for Adam and Eve. In other words, the devil said God did not have their best interest in mind.

In the beginning he made accusations against God. In the last book of the Bible, the Book of Revelation, we find that the devil also accuses believers.

> Then I heard a loud voice in heaven say: The salvation and the power and the kingdom of our God and the authority of His Messiah have now come, because the accuser of our brothers has been thrown out: the one who accuses them before our God day and night (Revelation 12:10 HCSB).

He accuses those who have believed in Jesus Christ.

6. THE TEMPTER

Satan is the one who tempts or entices people to sin. At Jesus' temptation, the devil is called "the tempter." We read.

> The tempter came and said to him, "If you are the Son of God, command these stones to become loaves of bread" (Matthew 4:3 NRSV).

He wants to bring out the worst in each of us. Consequently, he entices us to sin against God.

7. THE RULER OF THE DEMONS

Demons are evil spirits. They are most likely fallen angels. This ungodly personage is called the ruler of the demons. This gives the impression that he has these spirit-beings under his control.

We find this title used by the Pharisees of Jesus' day. The Bible says.

But the Pharisees said, "He casts out demons by the ruler of the demons" (Matthew 9:34 NKJV).

Interestingly, the Pharisees accused Jesus of casting out demons by the power of Satan, the ruler of the demons. They could not deny His miraculous work, so they had to attribute His power to something.

8. BEELZEBUL

Satan is known as Beelzebul, which means "lord of the flies," or "lord of dung." We read of this in Matthew's gospel.

But when the Pharisees heard it, they said, "It is only by Beelzebul, the ruler of the demons, that this fellow casts out the demons" (Matthew 12:24 NRSV).

This is a title that certainly belongs to this evil being,!

9. THE EVIL ONE

Satan is also called the "evil one." We find this title used by the Lord Jesus in one of His parables. He described the devil as follows.

The seeds that fell along the road are the people who hear the message about the kingdom, but don't understand it. Then the evil one comes and snatches the message from their hearts (Matthew 13:19 CEV).

Satan is indeed evil. In this particular instance, he is the "evil one." This indicates that he is the head or authority over all things which are evil.

10. THE ENEMY

He is the enemy of humanity. Jesus called this personage the "enemy" when He explained the parable of the wheat and the weeds to His disciples. We read.

He answered, "The one who sowed the good seed is the Son of Man. The field is the world, and the good seed stands for the people of the kingdom. The weeds are the people of the evil one, and the enemy who sows them is the devil. The harvest is the end of the age, and the harvesters are angels" (Matthew 13:39 NIV).

The devil is the archenemy of humanity. Indeed, this being is our chief enemy.

11. LIAR

Jesus made it clear that Satan, this evil personage, is always a liar. Liar, therefore, is an appropriate title. John recorded Jesus saying the following to the religious leaders of His day.

> You are of your father the Devil, and you want to carry out your father's desires. He was a murderer from the beginning and has not stood in the truth, because there is no truth in him. When he tells a lie, he speaks from his own nature, because he is a liar and the father of liars (John 8:44 HCSB).

There is no truth in him. In this comparison he is the opposite of Jesus. Jesus is the "truth," while the devil is the "lie."

12. FATHER OF LIES

In addition, we find that the devil is the one who originated lies. Jesus said the following about where lies originated.

> You are from your father the devil . . . . When he lies, he speaks according to his own nature, for he is a liar and the father of lies (John 8:44 NRSV).

The Contemporary English Version reads this way.

Your father is the devil, and you do exactly what he wants. . . There is nothing truthful about him. He speaks on his own, and everything he says is a lie. Not only is he a liar himself, but he is also the father of all lies (John 8:44 CEV).

The point is clear. Indeed, all lies stem from him.

13. MURDERER

This unrighteous fallen personage is also a murderer. Jesus accused him as being a murderer from the very beginning.

You are of your father the Devil, and you want to carry out your father's desires. He was a murderer from the beginning (John 8:44 HCSB).

From the very beginning, this evil being has been a murderer.

14. THE RULER OF THIS WORLD

Satan is the ruler of this world-system in the sense that the world is still characterized by sin. Jesus said the following words about him on the night of His betrayal.

I cannot speak with you much longer, because the ruler of this world is coming. But he has no power over me. I obey my Father, so that everyone in the world might know that I love him (John 14:30,31 CEV).

This title suggests that he is the major influence over our world.

Elsewhere, Scripture teaches that the whole world is in his power. We read the following words in First John.

We know that we are of God, and the whole world lies *under the sway of* the wicked one (1 John 5:19 NKJV).

This present world-system is under his control.

15. THE GOD OF THIS AGE

The devil is called the "god of this age." When Paul wrote to the Corinthians he used this title in describing this being.

> The god of this age has blinded the minds of unbelievers, so that they cannot see the light of the gospel that displays the glory of Christ, who is the image of God (2 Corinthians 4:4 NIV).

Satan is the god of this evil age. This wicked world worships and follows him in the sense that it gives the highest importance to all things evil. Money, lust, and greed are all aspects of the world-system in which the devil is god.

16. AN ANGEL OF LIGHT

This being, who is completely evil, appears as an angel of light. The Apostle Paul also wrote to the Corinthians.

> And it is no wonder. Even Satan tries to make himself look like an angel of light. So why does it seem strange for Satan's servants to pretend to do what is right? Someday they will get exactly what they deserve (2 Corinthians 11:14,15 CEV).

This corrupt personage masquerades as an angel of light. In other words, he pretends to be something which he is not.

17. BELIAL

The idea behind Belial is "vileness." This title may be applied to the devil, but only by implication. Paul wrote to the Corinthians.

> And what accord has Christ with Belial? Or what part has a believer with an unbeliever? (2 Corinthians 6:15 NKJV).

The New Living Translation puts the verse this way.

What harmony can there be between Christ and the Devil? How can a believer be a partner with an unbeliever? (2 Corinthians 6:15 NLT).

This translation sees this as a reference to the devil himself. Belial was seemingly a popular name for the devil at Jesus' time.

18. THE RULER OVER THE AUTHORITY (KINGDOM) OF THE AIR

Satan is the authority over this present evil world-system. Indeed, he rules over it. Paul emphasized this when he wrote to the Ephesians. He said.

> As for you, you were dead in your transgressions and sins, in which you used to live when you followed the ways of this world and of the ruler of the kingdom of the air, the spirit who is now at work in those who are disobedient (Ephesians 2:1-2 NIV).

Satan is the personage behind our present world system. Of course, the good news from Scripture is that this world-system will not always exist. Jesus will return and replace it with His kingdom, a kingdom based in righteousness.

19. THE ADVERSARY

This being stands in opposition to everything holy. In fact, the word "Satan" means the "adversary." Peter explained him in this manner.

> Be sober! Be on the alert! Your adversary the Devil is prowling around like a roaring lion, looking for anyone he can devour (1 Peter 5:8 HCSB).

He is the adversary of humans. Fortunately, we believers have the Lord to protect us from this adversary who wishes to devour us.

20. A ROARING LION

He is likened to a lion which goes about seeking its prey. Indeed, he wants to devour people. Peter wrote this description of him.

> Keep your mind clear, and be alert. Your opponent the devil is prowling around like a roaring lion as he looks for someone to devour (1 Peter 5:8 God's Word).

The devil is compared to a roaring lion. This analogy certainly gives us the idea that he is a ferocious being.

21. THE ANGEL OVER THE ABYSS

In the Book of Revelation, there is an angel referred to as the "angel over the abyss," or the "angel over the bottomless pit." He is also described as a "king." Scripture says.

> They had as king over them the angel of the Abyss, whose name in Hebrew is Abaddon and in Greek is Apollyon (that is, Destroyer). (Revelation 9:11 NIV).

There is some question as to whether this is a description of Satan, or merely a powerful evil angel. Whoever this personage may be, he has authority over this pit.

22. APOLLYON AND ABADDON

This angel in charge of the bottomless pit is called Apollyon and Abaddon. In the Book of Revelation it describes him in this manner.

> Their king was the angel in charge of the deep pit. In Hebrew his name was Abaddon, and in Greek it was Apollyon (Revelation 9:11 CEV).

The idea behind these terms is "destroyer." Satan has been filled with hatred against God from the beginning, and has attempted to destroy every good thing that the Lord has done. Again, this reference may be referring to a particular evil angel rather than the devil.

23. THE DRAGON

This personage who became the devil is also called "the dragon." In the Book of Revelation, it identifies this dragon with the devil, Satan.

> The great dragon was hurled down—that ancient ser-
> pent called the devil, or Satan, who leads the whole world
> astray. He was hurled to the earth, and his angels with him
> (Revelation 12:9 NIV).

The term dragon brings to mind a creature which is frightful.

24. THE ANCIENT SERPENT (THE OLD SERPENT)

He is also known as the ancient, or old, serpent, or the old snake. The Book of Revelation says.

> So the great dragon was thrown out—the ancient serpent,
> who is called the Devil and Satan, the one who deceives the
> whole world. He was thrown to earth, and his angels with
> him (Revelation 12:9 HCSB).

This reminds us of the Garden of Eden, when Satan came to Eve in the form of a snake or serpent. It speaks of his cunning.

25. THE DECEIVER OF THE WHOLE WORLD

This evil being deceives the entire unbelieving world. The Bible says the following about his deception.

> So that huge dragon—the ancient serpent, the one called
> the devil and Satan, who deceives the whole world-was
> thrown down to the earth, and his angels along with him
> (Revelation 12:9 NET).

Deception is what this unrighteous being is all about. In fact, he is the master deceiver.

26. THE ACCUSER OF GOD'S PEOPLE

This evil personage constantly makes accusations against God's people. We also read in the Book of Revelation.

> Then I heard a loud voice shouting across the heavens, "It has happened at last—the salvation and power and kingdom of our God, and the authority of his Christ! For the Accuser has been thrown down to earth—the one who accused our brothers and sisters before our God day and night" (Revelation 12:10 NLT).

He accuses the people of God both night and day. In other words, his accusations never cease.

In sum, these are the different titles and descriptions which the Scripture gives of this fallen being. He truly is completely evil.

SUMMARY TO QUESTION 18
WHAT ARE SOME OF THE DIFFERENT TITLES OF SATAN?

The devil is the enemy of the human race. He is the one who attempts to cause humanity to turn away from the living God. His goal is to draw people away from the Lord and His truth.

In addition, this personage is constantly at war with God's people. He is specifically trying to defeat us in the spiritual realm. Therefore, it is important to know the character of the one in which we are fighting.

When we study the Scripture, we find that there are a number of names attributed to Satan, the devil. These names give us some insight into his character, as well as the various ways in which he deals with humanity.

Though not every one of these names may be a specific reference to this personage, many of these names have been ascribed to him.

This being is called such things as Satan, day star, son of the morning, the anointed cherub, the devil, tempter, ruler of demons, Beelzebub, the evil one, enemy, liar, father of lies, murderer, ruler of this world, god of this age, angel of light, Belial, ruler and authority over the air, adversary, roaring lion, the angel of the abyss, Apollyon, Abaddon, dragon, the ancient serpent, deceiver of the whole world, and accuser of God's people.

Each of these names points to his ungodly character. The chief characteristics we find in this creature are his hostility, cunning, power, and evil intent toward God and His people.

Now that we know the various things which he is called, we can have a better idea of what to be on guard against. Indeed, we know our enemy and the ways in which he operates. By examining these various names or titles which are given to him, we understand who we are fighting, as well as how he is attempting to lead us astray.

QUESTION 19

Does Isaiah Speak
Of Satan's Fall? (Isaiah 14)

There is a passage in the Book of Isaiah that may refer to the fall of the created spirit-being who became Satan, the devil. It reads as follows.

> How you have fallen from heaven, morning star, son of the dawn! You have been cast down to the earth, you who once laid low the nations! You said in your heart, "I will ascend to the heavens; I will raise my throne above the stars of God; I will sit enthroned on the mount of assembly, on the utmost heights of Mount Zaphon. I will ascend above the tops of the clouds; I will make myself like the Most High" (Isaiah 14:12-15 NIV).

In the immediate context of Isaiah, the subject is the King of Babylon. Yet there seems to be a sinister person behind the king to whom this passage is referring. Many Bible students think that it refers to the original fall of the highest ranked created being who became the devil.

If this is true, then we can learn more things about this evil personage. We can make the following observations.

THERE ARE FIVE "I WILLS" IN THIS PASSAGE

There are five different times in this passage when the personage asserted his own will, rather than the will of God.

131

1. I WILL ASCEND TO HEAVEN

Ascending to heaven has the idea of being like God. The Bible says that Jesus ascended to heaven in the presence of His disciples. The Book of Acts records.

> And when he had said these things, as they were looking on, he was lifted up, and a cloud took him out of their sight. And while they were gazing into heaven as he went, behold, two men stood by them in white robes, and said, "Men of Galilee, why do you stand looking into heaven? This Jesus, who was taken up from you into heaven, will come in the same way as you saw him go into heaven" (Acts 1:9-11 ESV).

While Jesus actually ascended into God's presence, this being wanted to be like God. However, he was just a pretender.

2. I WILL EXALT MY THRONE

Pride is seen here in the exaltation of self, rather than the Lord. God is the only One who is worthy to sit on the heavenly throne. We read the following in the Book of Revelation about this.

> The angel showed me a river that was crystal clear, and its waters gave life. The river came from the throne where God and the Lamb were seated (Revelation 22:1 CEV).

This personage wanted to be exalted above the stars of God. The term "stars" could symbolize the angels, other created beings whom the Lord had made.

This is a terrible sin in the eyes of the Lord. Indeed, pride is put first on the list of things which God hates. We read about this in Proverbs. It says.

> There are six things the LORD hates, seven that are detestable to him: haughty eyes, a lying tongue, hands that shed innocent blood (Proverbs 6:16,17 NIV).

"Haughty eyes" is an idiomatic expression for "pride." The Lord hates pride, the sin of this created being who became the devil.

3. I WILL SIT UPON THE MOUNT OF CONGREGATION

The governing of heaven is a position that belongs only to the Lord. We read about this in the Book of Isaiah.

> In days to come the mountain of the LORD's house shall be established as the highest of the mountains, and shall be raised above the hills; all the nations shall stream to it (Isaiah 2:2 NRSV).

This evil being wanted to take for himself that which belongs to the Lord, and to Him alone. He wanted to exercise authority which was not rightly his.

4. I WILL ASCEND ABOVE THE HEIGHTS OF THE CLOUDS

Again, there is the personal desire for exaltation. Clouds in Scripture often represent the glory of God. This particular created being wanted exaltation above the glory of God. However, Jesus is the One who will be exalted.

Paul wrote the following to the Philippians about how Jesus Christ is exalted by God the Father. He explained it this way.

> Therefore God also highly exalted him and gave him the name that is above every name (Philippians 2:9 NRSV).

God exalted Jesus Christ. He has been given a name which is above every name. On the other hand, this evil being only wants to exalt himself.

5. I WILL MAKE MYSELF LIKE THE MOST HIGH

This personage wishes to be like the Lord, but there is only one "God Most High." In the Book of Genesis, the Bible refers to the God of Scripture as the "God Most High."

Melchizedek blessed Abram with this blessing: "Blessed be Abram by God Most High, Creator of heaven and earth. . . . Abram replied, "I have solemnly promised the LORD, God Most High, Creator of heaven and earth" (Genesis 14:19,22 NLT).

There can only be one "God Most High." This created being, who became Satan, the adversary, does not qualify.

In sum, these five "I wills" seem to give us an indication of what motivated this created spirit-being to stage a rebellion against the Lord.

NEW TESTAMENT CONNECTIONS WITH THIS PASSAGE

This passage in Isaiah has been linked with two verses in the New Testament: Luke 10:18 and Revelation 12:8.

And he [Jesus] said to them, "I saw Satan fall like lightning from heaven" (Luke 10:18 ESV).

Note that Jesus speaks of the fall of Satan *from* the location of heaven, not that he is the "most high."

In the Book of Revelation, we read another passage that speaks of his downward ascent. The Bible says.

And the dragon lost the battle and was forced out of heaven (Revelation 12:8 NLT).

The timing of these two statements does not seem to speak of Satan's original fall. Jesus' statement does not give us any idea as to when this fall from heaven occurred, and the statement in Revelation is dealing with events that are still in the future.

Therefore, this particular casting down to the earth has still yet to take place.

In sum, this passage in Isaiah does seem to give us an indication of what took place when this particular created being rebelled against God and therefore became the devil. Indeed, it gives us insight into his motivation; he wanted to be like God.

SUMMARY TO QUESTION 19
DOES ISAIAH SPEAK OF SATAN'S FALL?

In the immediate context of Isaiah chapter fourteen the subject is the King of Babylon. However, behind this earthly king appears to be the personage of the created spirit-being who became the devil.

This can be seen by some of the statements that seemingly could not be referring to the earthly king of Babylon. If this is true, then we gain insight into the motivation for the original sin of this created being who became the devil. We find the following things stated in these verses.

Five times in this passage the words, "I will" are used. This indicates the sin of pride caused the downfall of this personage. Instead of wanting to do the will of God, this being wanted to exert his own will.

We also find that this personage wanted to ascend to heaven. Heaven, in this sense, is the place where God uniquely dwells. The desire to ascend to heaven speaks of the desire to be like God. None of us can attain this.

This creature also wanted to exalt his throne. Instead of submitting to the rightful king, this personage was lifted up with pride.

Furthermore, he also wanted to sit on the mount of the congregation. This means that he wanted a position of authority that did not belong to him.

The passage also says that he wanted to ascend above the clouds. This shows a desire to be exalted to a place higher than he deserved.

Finally, we find that this creature wanted to be like the "Most High God." Yet, there is only one God and nobody, whether a created heavenly being or a human being, can be like Him.

All of this seems to be a description of the personage who fell from his original perfect state and became the devil. Indeed, the description does not seem to fit a mere mortal.

Therefore, while it is not certain that this passage in Isaiah is speaking of the fall of Satan, it does seem to be consistent with the rest of Scripture.

Is Ezekiel Speaking Of Satan Or The King Of Tyre? (Ezekiel 28)

In the Book of Ezekiel, there is a description of someone called the "King of Tyre." Though there was an actual historical person who was this particular king, the description the Bible gives of this person seems to go far beyond this human leader.

Indeed, while in context, Ezekiel was first speaking about the historical King of Tyre, he seemingly moved into the dateless past with a description of the original fall of Satan. The passage in question reads as follows.

> Moreover, the word of the Lord came to me: "Son of man, raise a lamentation over the king of Tyre, and say to him, Thus says the Lord God: "You were the signet of perfection, full of wisdom and perfect in beauty. You were in Eden, the garden of God; every precious stone was your covering, sardius, topaz, and diamond, beryl, onyx, and jasper, sapphire, emerald, and carbuncle; and crafted in gold were your settings and your engravings. On the day that you were created they were prepared. You were an anointed guardian cherub. I placed you; you were on the holy mountain of God; in the midst of the stones of fire you walked. You were blameless in your ways from the day you were created, till unrighteousness was found in you. In the abundance of your trade you

were filled with violence in your midst, and you sinned; so I cast you as a profane thing from the mountain of God, and I destroyed you, O guardian cherub, from the midst of the stones of fire. Your heart was proud because of your beauty; you corrupted your wisdom for the sake of your splendor. I cast you to the ground; I exposed you before kings, to feast their eyes on you. By the multitude of your iniquities, in the unrighteousness of your trade you profaned your sanctuaries; so I brought fire out from your midst; it consumed you, and I turned you to ashes on the earth in the sight of all who saw you. All who know you among the peoples are appalled at you; you have come to a dreadful end and shall be no more forever (Ezekiel 28:12-19 ESV).

In this long passage, this is how the Bible describes the punishment that will come upon the king of Tyre. In verses 12-15, he is described before his fall into sin and from verses 16-19, his sin is described. We can make the following observations.

IS THIS A DESCRIPTION OF THE FALL OF SATAN?

Admittedly, this is a difficult passage to interpret. There are many who believe that this is a description of the account of the original fall of the personage who became the devil, Satan. While some of the descriptions given may fit the historical king of Tyre, others certainly do not seem to. These include the expressions: "perfect in beauty," "you were in Eden," "you were on the holy mountain of God," "you were an anointed guardian cherub" and "you were blameless."

These images would not literally fit the actual King of Tyre. Therefore, they are most likely to be understood as statements about the original fall of the created being who became the devil.

This type of double reference is not unique to this passage of Scripture. We also find references to David in the Old Testament where David's greater Son, the Messiah, is actually the subject.

Therefore, it is certainly consistent with the rest of the Bible to allow a double reference here.

WHAT CAN WE LEARN ABOUT SATAN?

If this does describe the original fall of Satan, then we can learn the following things about this created being.

1. HE WAS FULL OF WISDOM AND PERFECT IN BEAUTY

When originally created by God, this personage, like everything else God created, was perfect. Not only that, he seemed to have been especially beautiful. In other words, he was one-of-a-kind.

2. HE LIVED IN EDEN

This Eden seemingly existed at a far earlier time than the Garden of Eden that God created on the earth. The description given here could hardly refer to the earthly Garden of Eden.

Indeed, in the Garden of Eden, as described in the Book of Genesis, there is no reference to gold or precious stones. The description given here in Ezekiel is more reminiscent of the New Jerusalem, found in Revelation 21-22, than the Garden of Eden. The New Jerusalem will be the place where redeemed believers live.

3. HE WAS THE ANOINTED CHERUB THAT COVERED

He is called the "anointed cherub." This particular description indicates that this created being held a position of superiority over all the other created beings. The cherubim, along with the seraphim, seem to be the highest ranked of all the heavenly beings. Since he was the "anointed cherub," it seemingly speaks of the highest position among the cherubim. In other words, this being was the "highest of the highest."

The phrase "that covered" reminds us that the cherubim overshadowed the Ark of the Covenant. This was a position which was next to the presence of God. All these things seem to add up to say that this personage had the highest rank in the universe of any created being, far above the angels.

This could also explain why certain angels followed him in his initial rebellion against the Lord. Indeed, if he was the highest ranking created being in the universe, the angels may have been influenced by his beauty, his wisdom and his position.

4. HE WAS IN GOD'S HOLY MOUNTAIN

The statement here refers to the unique dwelling place of God, His visible glory. This personage was in the immediate presence of the Lord. He was surrounded by the brilliance of heaven. This was indeed a privileged and exalted position.

5. HE WALKED IN THE MIDST OF STONES OF FIRE

The stones of fire seem to speak of the nearness to God's throne. When Moses brought Aaron, Nadab, Abihu, and seventy of the elders up to Mount Sinai to see God's presence, we read the following.

> There they saw the God of Israel. Under his feet there seemed to be a pavement of brilliant sapphire, as clear as the heavens . . . The Israelites at the foot of the mountain saw an awesome sight. The awesome glory of the LORD on the mountaintop looked like a devouring fire Exodus (24:10,17 NLT).

This description could be the same as the stones of fire that we find here in Ezekiel. If so, it would indicate the nearness this personage had to the throne of God.

6. HE WAS PERFECT IN ALL HIS WAYS UNTIL HIS FALL

The perfection of this creature is again stressed. There was no defect in him until he chose to sin. He, like everything which God had created, was absolutely perfect.

7. HE WAS LIFTED UP WITH PRIDE BECAUSE OF HIS BEAUTY

Because of his great beauty, this creature was lifted up with pride. Scripture has much to say on the subject of pride.

> Pride precedes a disaster, and an arrogant attitude precedes a fall (Proverbs 16:18 God's Word).

Pride always leads to disaster. His fall, because of pride, should be a lesson to us all.

8. HIS WISDOM WAS CORRUPTED BECAUSE OF HIS BRIGHTNESS

The great wisdom of this personage had now been corrupted. Obviously it was insanity for this creature to think that he could somehow overcome the Creator.

9. HE WAS THROWN OUT OF THE MOUNTAIN OF GOD

This possibly speaks of either the initial punishment of this created being when he was banished from his exalted position.

It may be speaking of his future punishment when he will be thrown down to the earth. This will take place immediately before Jesus Christ comes again. Either way, his punishment is certain.

10. HIS POSITION WAS DEGRADED WHEN HE SINNED

No longer would this personage hold a lofty position. He will never again be spoken of as the "anointed cherub" or whatever other title he had previously held.

11. HE BECAME AN ENEMY OF HUMANITY

Now this beautiful created being becomes Satan, the adversary, the enemy of humanity.

Therefore, if this description is of the original fall of the personage that became Satan, the adversary, and this does seem likely, then we have insight into who he was, what he did, and to some extent, why he rebelled against the Lord.

Again we stress, not every Bible commentator believes this is a description of the fall of Satan. They see it as merely a poetic description of an evil earthly king.

SUMMARY TO QUESTION 20
IS EZEKIEL SPEAKING OF SATAN OR THE KING OF TYRE?

In Ezekiel 28, there is a description of the fall of the King of Tyre. From this passage there also seems to be a description of the original fall of Satan, the created being who became the devil.

However, not all interpreters agree with this interpretation. They believe it refers solely to the King of Tyre. Therefore, the various things said about him are hyperbole; the use of exaggeration as a rhetorical device or figure of speech.

Yet, if it does refer to Satan and his fall, then we learn much about him in this passage.

To begin with, he was the "anointed cherub" who had a special place next to the throne of God. In other words, his position was like none other in the universe.

Because of his special place in God's order, and his extraordinary beauty, he was lifted up with pride. This caused him to rebel against God.

This being did not get away with his sin. He was immediately judged by being thrown out of God's presence. While he is still allowed to do his evil work, he is awaiting his ultimate punishment.

He is now the enemy of the human race. Indeed, this personage is the one who is behind all evil which exists.

These facts seem to be consistent with what we know about this evil personage from the rest of Scripture. Yet because there is no specific reference to a supernatural creature in this passage, we cannot be absolutely certain that it speaks of Satan's fall.

QUESTION 21

Why Did God Use The King Of Babylon And The King Of Tyre To Illustrate The Fall Of Satan?

As we indicated, not every Bible student agrees that statements in Isaiah 14 and Ezekiel 28 refer to the original fall of Satan. They could simply be speaking about these two ancient kings in a poetic fashion. The descriptions of them would be merely exaggerations used for emphasis. In other words, figures of speech, hyperbole.

If, however, they do contain references to his original fall, then why were the King of Tyre and the King of Babylon first addressed? Why choose these two earthly kings to illustrate the downfall of the created being who became the devil?

There are a number of points that need to be made in answering this question.

1. THIS IS NOT AN UNCOMMON PRACTICE

To begin with, it is not uncommon in Scripture for the writer to move from descriptions of earthly events to heavenly events; when there were some parallels between the two.

For example, Psalm 45 first describes an earthly king, but then goes on to describe the Messiah; the King who will come from heaven. Therefore, the move from these earthly kings, to the fall of the personage who became Satan, is consistent with other parts of Scripture.

2. THERE MAY HAVE BEEN A PRACTICAL PURPOSE

But why were the King of Tyre and the King of Babylon first addressed? It is possible that the prophet did it this way for a very practical purpose.

The King of Tyre and the King of Babylon had both claimed worship as some sort of divine being (see Daniel 3:1-12). They made their subjects bow down to them. They wanted to be treated as God by their people.

3. GOD GAVE A WARNING

God, therefore, used these prophets to warn against this blasphemy by going back to the dateless past. It recounted the story when a created being originally rebelled against Him and became the devil, the adversary. The personage who began the rebellion did so by saying, "I will be like God." Therefore, the behavior of these earthly kings, like that of this created being so long ago, was rooted in the attempt to be as God.

4. THERE IS A LESSON TO BE LEARNED

There was an obvious lesson in all of this. If God had originally punished the blasphemy and pride of this mighty being who rebelled against Him, then He will certainly punish any human king who himself claims to be God. In other words, they should learn from the past events.

We also find that Satan had already attempted the same thing with Adam and Eve. Through the serpent he said the following to Eve.

> God knows that your eyes will be opened when you eat it. You will become just like God, knowing everything, both good and evil (Genesis 3:5 NLT).

This promise of Satan, that they would be as God in some sense, can be compared to the statement found in Isaiah where this personage himself wanted to be like God.

I will climb to the highest heavens and be like the Most High (Isaiah 14:14 NLT).

The being wanted to be like the only God, the One who has no peer.

5. THE TEMPTATION OF JESUS ILLUSTRATES THIS

His pride, arrogance, and desire to be worshipped continued as he tempted the Lord Jesus. Matthew records him saying the following to Christ.

"I will give it all to you," he said, "if you will only kneel down and worship me" (Matthew 4:9 NLT).

Satan wanted the One who deserved worship, the Lord Jesus, to bow down and worship him. Jesus, of course, refused to do this.

6. HE IS THE GOD OF THIS AGE

Satan is also called "the god of this age," "the god of this world," in Scripture. The Apostle Paul gave this description of him to the Corinthians.

The god of this age has blinded the minds of unbelievers, so that they cannot see the light of the gospel of the glory of Christ, who is the image of God (2 Corinthians 4:4 NIV).

Therefore, Satan has been consistent from the beginning in attempting to be like God, and tempting others to do the same.

7. HE WILL RECEIVE TEMPORARY SATISFACTION

This long-held ambition of Satan will be temporarily satisfied when the inhabitants of the earth will worship him, and his own representative the final Antichrist. We read of this in the Book of Revelation.

So they worshiped the dragon who gave authority to the beast; and they worshiped the beast, saying, "Who *is* like the beast? Who is able to make war with him?" (Revelation 13:4 NKJV).

For a short period of time, his desire to be worshipped will be satisfied. Yet it will indeed come to a bitter end for him.

In sum, God seemingly used the original fall of this personage who became the devil to teach two earthly kings the uselessness of trying to be like God.

In addition, it gives us some insight into this beautiful wise created being who fell from his lofty position.

SUMMARY TO QUESTION 21
WHY DID GOD USE THE KING OF BABYLON AND THE KING OF TYRE TO ILLUSTRATE THE FALL OF SATAN?

There are two passages in the Old Testament which describe the judgment of pagan kings; the King of Tyre and the King of Babylon.

However, these passages seem to be speaking of much more than that. Seemingly, God used the example of two pagan kings, those of Tyre and Babylon, to illustrate the original fall of the created being who became the devil. There are a number of reasons as to why this was done.

It looks like both the King of Tyre and the King of Babylon claimed to be some sort of heavenly being who was worthy of worship. This is why they were used to illustrate the fall of the personage who became the devil. It is not uncommon for the Scripture to use the same passage to describe both earthly and heavenly truths.

If this is the case, then we find that the desire of these kings to be worshipped was similar to the desire of this beautiful wise being who became the devil. He wanted to receive the worship that was due to God and to Him alone.

This is consistent with what we know of Satan. We find that in Jesus' temptation by the devil that this evil being wanted Christ to worship him. Obviously this sinful creature desires worship which he does not deserve. Jesus refused to worship him.

Consequently, the fall of this personage from his lofty position, is a lesson for all who would attempt to take the place of God. While they may receive temporary satisfaction from placing themselves in a position of receiving worship from others, ultimately they will be judged and punished.

Indeed, there is only one God who exists, and one God who deserves worship. All of those who attempt to rob Him of His glory will be punished.

How Has The Devil Attempted To Thwart God's Plan Of The Ages?

The created spirit-being who became the devil has tried to thwart the plan of God from the very beginning of time. He has attempted to do it in at least five different ways. Satan's five target areas of destruction have been as follows.

1. THE HUMAN RACE

2. THE NATION ISRAEL

3. THE PROMISED LINE

4. JESUS CHRIST

5. THE NEW TESTAMENT CHURCH

The following observations can be made about these direct attacks of Satan.

TARGET 1: THE HUMAN RACE

When God created humanity, He made them according to His image and likeness. Adam and Eve were created perfect, and were placed in a perfect environment. There was no sin or evil anywhere upon the earth.

Yet Satan, through the serpent, tempted them to sin, and this first couple gave in to the temptation. The race that was originally created perfect would now have to be judged. Adam and Eve were banished from the Garden of Eden and the children born of humans would now be born with a sinful nature.

Sin continued to have its way. Satan attempted to corrupt the human race to the point where God would destroy everything that He had made. It almost came to that. The Bible says the following conditions prevailed upon the earth.

> Then the LORD saw that the wickedness of man was great in the earth, and that every intent of the thoughts of his heart was only evil continually. And the LORD was sorry that He had made man on the earth, and He was grieved in His heart (Genesis 6:5,6 NKJV).

God sent a Flood to destroy the entire world, except for eight persons. The human race was spared Satan's attempt to annihilate it.

TARGET 2: THE NATION ISRAEL

A second target of the devil has been the nation Israel. Four thousand years ago, God gave a man named Abram a number of promises. We read of some of them in the following passage.

> Then the LORD told Abram, "Leave your country, your relatives, and your father's house, and go to the land that I will show you. I will cause you to become the father of a great nation. I will bless you and make you famous, and I will make you a blessing to others. I will bless those who bless you and curse those who curse you. All the families of the earth will be blessed through you" (Genesis 12:1-3 NLT).

Among other things, God promised that the descendants of Abraham would exist forever. If the nation that came from Abraham's descendants, Israel, were ever annihilated, then the Word of God would be untrue.

It is for this reason that Satan has paid special attention to Abraham's descendants in his attempt to thwart the plan of God. He has wanted to destroy them from the beginning.

AN ATTEMPT TO DESTROY THE JEWS

In the Book of Esther, we have an example of the attempted destruction of the entire nation. In fact, a decree went out to destroy all the Jews.

> Then the king's scribes were summoned on the thirteenth day of the first month, and an edict, according to all that Haman commanded, was written to the king's satraps and to the governors over all the provinces and to the officials of all the peoples, to every province in its own script and every people in its own language. It was written in the name of King Ahasuerus and sealed with the king's signet ring. Letters were sent by couriers to all the king's provinces with instruction to destroy, to kill, and to annihilate all Jews, young and old, women and children, in one day, the thirteenth day of the twelfth month, which is the month of Adar, and to plunder their goods. A copy of the document was to be issued as a decree in every province by proclamation to all the peoples to be ready for that day (Esther 3:12-14 ESV).

God providentially intervened and saved the nation from annihilation. If Satan had been able to destroy the Jews, then the promises of God would not be true. However, he was not allowed to do this.

TARGET 3: THE LINE OF THE MESSIAH

After sin entered into our world, the Lord began to promise that He would send a Deliverer, a Messiah who would save the people from their sins. God also promised to judge Satan through the promised Messiah.

From now on, you and the woman will be enemies, and your offspring and her offspring will be enemies. He will crush your head, and you will strike his heel (Genesis 3:15 NLT).

The Messiah was to be the One who would defeat the serpent, to crush his head.

Among other things, God selected one particular family line from where the Messiah would arise. From the beginning, Satan has attempted to destroy this chosen line of the Messiah. Hence, if the chosen line were destroyed, then God's plan would be thwarted.

THIS HAS BEEN FROM THE BEGINNING

He has indeed persisted in this effort from the very beginning. Cain, the first child born to Adam and Eve, killed his brother Abel. The Bible says of Cain.

We must not be like Cain who was from the evil one and murdered his brother. And why did he murder him? Because his own deeds were evil and his brother's righteous (1 John 3:12 NRSV).

When Abel was killed, another son was born to Adam and Eve. His name was Seth. He was in the promised line of the Deliverer. Throughout history, the devil has continued his attempt, with no success, to destroy the promised line. Again, we have his failure documented.

TARGET 4: JESUS CHRIST

A fourth way, in which Satan has attempted to stop the plan of God, is in the mission of God the Son, Jesus Christ. From the time before His birth, Satan attempted to keep Jesus from fulfilling His destiny.

THE SLAUGHTER OF THE INNOCENTS

Therefore, we find Satan behind the evil work of King Herod who ordered the slaughtering of the innocent male babies in Bethlehem. In attempting to kill the baby Jesus, Satan was trying to keep Him from fulfilling His Messianic mission. The Bible says.

> When Herod realized that he had been outwitted by the Magi, he was furious, and he gave orders to kill all the boys in Bethlehem and its vicinity who were two years old and under, in accordance with the time he had learned from the Magi (Matthew 2:16 NIV).

The Lord has previously intervened by sending an angel to tell Joseph to take the Child with himself and Mary and flee to Egypt.

> When they had gone, an angel of the Lord appeared to Joseph in a dream. "Get up," he said, "take the child and his mother and escape to Egypt. Stay there until I tell you, for Herod is going to search for the child to kill him." So he got up, took the child and his mother during the night and left for Egypt, where he stayed until the death of Herod. And so was fulfilled what the Lord had said through the prophet: "Out of Egypt I called my son" (Matthew 2:13-15 NIV).

Therefore, the plan of Herod to kill Jesus, energized by Satan, was thwarted. However, this would not be the last attempt to keep Jesus from fulfilling His mission.

THE FORTY DAY TEMPTATION OF THE LORD JESUS

Not being able to kill Jesus, the devil tried another tactic. At the forty day temptation of Jesus, Satan attempted to thwart God's plan by having Jesus worship him. We read of this in the Gospel of Matthew.

> And he said to Him, "All these things I will give You if You will fall down and worship me" (Matthew 4:9 NKJV).

Jesus refused, and Satan was again defeated.

HE WANTED JESUS TO BYPASS THE CROSS

His attempts to stop Jesus continued. When Simon Peter attempted to get Jesus to bypass the cross, Jesus rebuked him, and declared that it was Satan who was behind such talk. We read the following words in Matthew.

> And Peter took him aside and began to rebuke him, saying, "God forbid it, Lord! This must never happen to you." But he turned and said to Peter, "Get behind me, Satan! You are a stumbling block to me; for you are setting your mind not on divine things but on human things" (Matthew 16:22-23 NRSV).

Satan, speaking through Peter, wanted Jesus to bypass the cross.

JESUS ACCOMPLISHED HIS MISSION

The mission that Jesus set out to do was indeed accomplished. Right before He died, He uttered words that showed He succeeded.

> When Jesus had tasted it, he said, "It is finished!" Then he bowed his head and gave up his spirit (John 19:30 NLT).

Jesus came as promised and fulfilled His mission. This was in spite of all the efforts by Satan. Again, this evil being was defeated in his plans.

TARGET 5: THE NEW TESTAMENT CHURCH

We find that Jesus predicted that He would build His church, His own community of believers. Furthermore, the Lord said that nothing would stop it.

> And I also say to you that you are Peter, and on this rock I will build My church, and the gates of Hades shall not prevail against it. (Matthew 16:18 NKJV).

Nothing could stop what the Lord has planned to do with His church. Nothing!

THE CHURCH CONTINUES TO CARRY JESUS' MESSAGE

The church, the true believers, in Jesus Christ, is carrying out His plan to spread His message throughout the earth. However, from the very first mention of the church by Jesus, a warning was given that Satan would oppose it. In fact, in his first letter to a church, Paul wrote of Satan hindering him.

> But since we were torn away from you, brothers, for a short time, in person not in heart, we endeavored the more eagerly and with great desire to see you face to face, because we wanted to come to you—I, Paul, again and again—but Satan hindered us (1 Thessalonians 2:17,18 ESV).

In addition, the Book of Acts, as well as two thousand years of church history, gives testimony to the fact that Satan has tried to stop its mission. Yet, like in all the other instances, the devil has failed to stop the plan of God.

Before Jesus Christ returns to the earth, the dragon, Satan, will still attempt to destroy the people of God. The Book of Revelation records that the dragon will attempt to destroy the offspring of the woman, Israel. We read the following.

> Then the dragon became furious with the woman and went off to make war on the rest of her offspring, on those who keep the commandments of God and hold to the testimony of Jesus. And he stood on the sand of the sea (Revelation 12:17 ESV).

However, like all other attempts, he will miserably fail. God's Word will not be contradicted.

In sum, we find that the devil has tried to stop God's plan of the ages in numerous ways. Yet each of these attempts has been met with failure. Indeed, they will continue to fail!

SUMMARY TO QUESTION 22
HOW HAS THE DEVIL ATTEMPTED TO THWART GOD'S PLAN OF THE AGES?

The Bible teaches that from the very beginning of life here upon the earth, Satan has attempted to thwart the plan of God. We find that he has done this in at least five different ways. They can be summed up as follows.

First, he has attempted to destroy the human race. Through the means of a snake, the devil tempted Adam and Eve to sin in the Garden of Eden. The perfect race was now imperfect. Yet God did not destroy humanity at that time but rather put in a plan to save us from our sinful state. Satan failed!

Next the devil targeted the chosen people; the nation of Israel. On a number of occasions, Satan tried to wipe out the entire population. If he could do this, then the promises of God would have been proven false. Yet Satan does not have this power and his attempts were again thwarted.

God also promised to send a Deliverer, a Messiah, to save His people. He specifically said that the Messiah would come through one particular family line, the line of David. The devil has tried to cut off the promised line of the Messiah. If he could accomplish this, then God's Word would be found to be untrue. However, the line of the Messiah was not ended and the Messiah came as predicted. Satan met another defeat.

This enemy of truth has sought to interfere with the mission of God the Son, Jesus Christ, when he came to this earth. First, he attempted to have Jesus killed immediately after He was born. The evil King Herod sent his soldiers to carry out this horrible deed. However, it failed.

Satan tempted the adult Jesus to bypass the cross by offering Him the kingdoms of this world in exchange for worship. However, it was the plan of God for Christ to die upon the cross. Jesus did not give in to the temptation. He completed the job God the Father had sent Him to do. Again we find another failure of the devil.

Finally, Satan has tried to destroy the work of God in the world today, the church. However, Jesus promised that His work through the church could not be destroyed. It has not. In fact, the work of the New Testament church continues to this very day. Again we see the failure of Satan to stop God's plan.

In each of these attempts, the devil has miserably failed. Satan has lost and the Lord has prevailed! This is documented for all to see.

Among other things, this further reinforces the fact that the Word of God is always true. God keeps his promises. Nothing in heaven or earth can stop this from happening.

In What Ways Did Jesus Achieve Victory Over The Devil?

One of the reasons for the coming of Jesus Christ to the earth was to destroy the works of the devil. John pointed this out when he wrote to the believers. He said.

> The person who lives a sinful life belongs to the devil, because the devil has been committing sin since the beginning. The reason that the Son of God appeared was to destroy what the devil does (1 John 3:8 God's Word).

The Bible speaks of a number of ways in which Jesus achieved victory over the devil. They include the following.

1. JESUS DEFEATED SATAN IN HIS SILENT YEARS

While this point is not usually made, it is nevertheless important to realize. Jesus defeated Satan in His silent years. Though He gave no sermons, performed no miracles, and was unknown to the public, He lived all these years without sin, doing everything that was pleasing to God the Father. At His baptism, the Father said of Jesus.

> And a voice from heaven said, "This is my Son, the Beloved, with whom I am well pleased" (Matthew 3:17 NRSV).

The Father was well-pleased with His Son. Well pleased with Jesus going about His everyday tasks as He was waiting for the time which He would be revealed to the world.

2. JESUS DEFEATED HIM AT THE TEMPTATION

Jesus did not succumb to the temptation of the devil (Matthew 4:1-11). Though Satan tested Jesus in various ways, there was no giving in to these temptations. Scripture says of Jesus.

> For we do not have a high priest who is unable to sympathize with our weaknesses, but one who in every respect has been tempted as we are, yet without sin (Hebrews 4:15 ESV).

Jesus never sinned, He never gave in to the temptations of the evil one. John also wrote about the sinlessness of Jesus. He said.

> And you know that He was manifested to take away our sins, and in Him there is no sin (1 John 3:5 NKJV).

Jesus did not give in to sin during the temptation.

3. JESUS DEFEATED THE DEVIL THROUGHOUT HIS PUBLIC MINISTRY

Jesus was also tempted during His public ministry. Amazingly, this took place by those who believed in Him, such as Simon Peter. In fact, we find that Peter wanted Jesus to bypass the cross, the very reason the Lord had come to the earth. Matthew records the conversation between the two of them.

> From that time Jesus began to show his disciples that he must go to Jerusalem and suffer many things from the elders and chief priests and scribes, and be killed, and on the third day be raised. And Peter took him aside and began to rebuke him, saying, "Far be it from you, Lord! This shall never happen to you." But he turned and said to Peter, "Get behind me, Satan! You are a hindrance to me. For you are not setting your mind on the things of God, but on the things of man (Matthew 16:21-23 ESV).

Jesus came to this earth for a specific purpose; to die for the sins of the world. Anyone or anything trying to hinder that destiny was working a work of Satan.

HE WAS TEMPTED BY HIS BROTHERS

The Lord Jesus was also tempted by those who did not believe in Him, such as His brothers. The Bible says that His half-brothers tempted Jesus to reveal Himself as the Messiah before the appointed time. We read the following in John's gospel.

> So his brothers said to him, "Leave here and go to Judea so that your disciples also may see the works you are doing; for no one who wants to be widely known acts in secret. If you do these things, show yourself to the world." (For not even his brothers believed in him.) (John 7:3-5 NRSV).

Note that they did not believe in Jesus at that time. We know that later at least two of them, James and Jude, did believe.

THE RELIGIOUS LEADERS TEMPTED JESUS

The religious leaders tempted Jesus for the purpose of bringing charges against Him. The Gospel of John says.

> They [the religious rulers] were trying to trap him into saying something they could use against him, but Jesus stooped down and wrote in the dust with his finger (John 8:6 NLT).

Jesus would not fall into their trap.

Each of these attempts failed while the Lord prevailed! At the end of His public ministry, Jesus was still without sin. He asked His disciples.

> Which of you convicts me of sin? If I tell the truth, why do you not believe me? (John 8:46 NRSV).

No sin could be found in Him. Indeed, He never sinned.

4. JESUS DEFEATED SATAN AT THE CROSS

The devil was also defeated by Jesus at the cross. Shortly before His death, Jesus said the following to His disciples.

> Judgment will come because the prince of this world has already been judged (John 16:11 NLT).

Jesus defeated Satan by His death on the cross of Calvary. The writer to the Hebrews would later put it this way.

> Since all of these sons and daughters have flesh and blood, Jesus took on flesh and blood to be like them. He did this so that by dying he would destroy the one who had power over death (that is, the devil) (Hebrews 2:14 God's Word).

Jesus' death destroyed the one who had the power over death.

5. JESUS DEFEATED SATAN AT THE RESURRECTION

Not only did Jesus give His life for the sins of the world, He rose from the dead. His resurrection from the dead broke Satan's power over fallen humanity. The Book of Revelation records the following words of Jesus.

> I am the First and the Last. I am the Living One; I was dead, and now look, I am alive for ever and ever! And I hold the keys of death and Hades (Revelation 1:17,18 HCSB).

Jesus, in coming back from the dead, has the final authority over death and the grave.

6. JESUS DEFEATED THE DEVIL IN THE LIVES OF BELIEVERS

Finally, Jesus has defeated Satan through the lives of those who have believed in Him. The Apostle Paul wrote the following to the church at Colosse.

He has delivered us from the domain of darkness and trans-
ferred us to the kingdom of his beloved Son, in whom we have
redemption, the forgiveness of sins (Colossians 1:13 ESV).

Through Jesus Christ, we have now been delivered from the power of
darkness.

The Bible says that believers look forward to the time when Satan's
defeat will be for all to see. Paul wrote.

The God of peace will soon crush Satan under your feet. The
grace of our Lord Jesus Christ be with you (Romans 16:20
ESV).

The lives of believers can be characterized by spiritual victory because
of the Lord's work on the cross. He has won the victory for us.

7. JESUS WILL BIND SATAN AT THE SECOND COMING

When Jesus Christ comes again, He will have Satan bound and
placed into the bottomless pit. We read the following in the Book of
Revelation.

Then I saw an angel coming down from heaven, holding in
his hand the key to the bottomless pit and a great chain.
And he seized the dragon, that ancient serpent, who is
the devil and Satan, and bound him for a thousand years
(Revelation 20:1,2 ESV).

The Second Coming of Jesus Christ will see the public defeat of Satan.
Indeed, everyone will know that this personage has been defeated.

8. JESUS WILL ACHIEVE FINAL VICTORY OVER SATAN THE LAKE OF FIRE - THE ULTIMATE PUNISHMENT

Eventually, Satan will be cast into the lake of fire, marking the final end
to his inglorious career. We read the following in the Book of Revelation.

And the devil who had deceived them was thrown into the lake of fire and sulfur, where the beast and the false prophet were, and they will be tormented day and night forever and ever (Revelation 20:10 NRSV).

This will be the final punishment for those who have rebelled against the Lord. Included in this punishment is the devil himself.

In sum, we find that Jesus has achieved victory over the devil in a number of important ways.

SUMMARY TO QUESTION 23
IN WHAT WAYS DID JESUS ACHIEVE VICTORY OVER THE DEVIL?

The defeat of Satan, by the Lord Jesus Christ, is complete. Indeed, Jesus has defeated the devil in many different ways.

For one thing, Jesus has defeated Satan through His silent years. Before He began His public ministry, Jesus lived in obscurity. Yet He remained obedient to the tasks given to Him.

At His baptism, God the Father testified that He was well pleased with Jesus. This was before He even began His public ministry. The silent years were victorious for Jesus.

At His forty-day temptation, Jesus thwarted the attempts of the devil to get Him to bypass God's plan and worship him instead. Jesus did not succumb to this temptation. Again we find that Jesus achieved victory over Satan.

Jesus' public ministry was also filled with temptations which came from the devil. Yet at the end of His ministry He could ask His disciples if they had ever seen Him sin. They had not because He never sinned. Another victory over the devil was achieved.

The death of Jesus, while momentarily looking like a defeat, was actually a victory over sin and death. Jesus took the punishment for the sins of the world upon Himself. Indeed, Satan was defeated at the cross!

Jesus' resurrection from the dead was another victory over the devil. Death could not hold Him. The resurrection demonstrates His ability to defeat death itself. It is another triumph over the devil by the Lord Jesus.

Jesus Christ continues to defeat Satan today through the lives of believers. Indeed, we have been delivered from the kingdom of darkness and transformed into the kingdom of light. Victory is, therefore, ongoing.

When Jesus Christ returns, He will have Satan bound in the bottomless pit and then eventually thrown into the lake of fire.

Jesus Christ, therefore, has thoroughly defeated Satan. This is an important biblical truth that each of us need to understand!

How Has Satan Attempted To Destroy The Church?

From the very beginning Satan has attempted to destroy the church which Jesus Christ has placed here upon the earth. The devil has done this in two ways, from the inside as well as from the outside. The evidence is as follows.

TACTIC 1: HE ATTACKS FROM WITHIN

One of the methods of Satan is to destroy the church from within. In fact, has done this in a number of ways. This includes having counterfeit believers who bring in false teaching.

1. COUNTERFEIT BELIEVERS WILL INFILTRATE THE CHURCH

Jesus warned about false believers mixing in with genuine believers when He explained one of His parables, the wheat and the weeds. We read about this in Matthew's gospel. It says the following.

> He answered, "The one who sows the good seed is the Son of Man. The field is the world, and the good seed is the sons of the kingdom. The weeds are the sons of the evil one, and the enemy who sowed them is the devil. The harvest is the end of the age, and the reapers are angels. Just as the weeds are gathered and burned with fire, so will it be at the end of the age" (Matthew 13:37-40 ESV).

Satan is the one who sows the bad seed. He does it by means of these false believers who infiltrate the church.

2. FALSE TEACHING WILL COME INTO THE CHURCH

These false believers will bring in false teaching. This will cause people to fall away from the faith. Paul wrote about this.

> Now the Spirit expressly says that in later times some will depart from the faith by devoting themselves to deceitful spirits and teachings of demons (1 Timothy 4:1 ESV).

We have been warned that many people will fall away from the faith by these false teachings. In this verse, it is called the "teachings of demons."

3. SATAN HAS HIS MINISTERS TO DO HIS WORK

Satan even has his own ministers to do his vile work. Paul warned about them in his letter to the Corinthians. He put it this way.

> And no wonder, for Satan himself masquerades as an angel of light. It is not surprising, then, if his servants also masquerade as servants of righteousness (2 Corinthians 11:14,15 NIV).

Consequently his ministers move in religious circles. They pose as ministers of righteousness but are, in reality, ministers of the devil.

4. HE HAS ALREADY INFILTRATED THE CHURCH

We find that these false teachers had already infiltrated the church in the early years of its existence. Jude wrote about this infiltration with the following words.

> I say this because some godless people have wormed their way in among you, saying that God's forgiveness allows us to live immoral lives. The fate of such people was determined long ago, for they have turned against our only Master and Lord, Jesus Christ (Jude 4 NLT).

The devil had already become part of the church. Unfortunately, he came to stay.

From the very beginning, Satan has been successful in getting Christians to sin. We read in the Book of Acts how he got a man named Ananias to lie to the Holy Spirit. We read.

> But Peter said, "Ananias, why has Satan filled your heart to lie to the Holy Spirit and keep back *part* of the price of the land for yourself?" (Acts 5:3 NKJV).

Unfortunately, during the entire history of the church, the devil has been successful in causing Christians to sin against the Lord.

Therefore, his attacks from within the church have caused many problems for believers.

TACTIC 2: HE DOES IT BY PERSECUTION

A second way in which Satan has attempted to destroy the work of the church is by means of persecution. From the very beginning, the devil has been the persecutor of the church of the living God. Jesus warned of this when He said the following.

> Do not fear what you are about to suffer. Behold, the devil is about to throw some of you into prison, that you may be tested, and for ten days you will have tribulation. Be faithful unto death, and I will give you the crown of life (Revelation 2:10 ESV).

Satan has constantly persecuted those who have believed in Jesus. This will continue until the Lord returns.

HE CANNOT ULTIMATELY WIN

Though the devil attempts to destroy the church from within and without, he knows that he cannot win. Sometimes he will win a particular battle with believers, but he will lose the war. The true believer in Jesus Christ will always prevail because Christ will see them through until the end. The Bible says the following about the righteous.

> They may trip seven times, but each time they will rise again. But one calamity is enough to lay the wicked low (Proverbs 24:16 NLT).

There is no chance that the devil will have the ultimate victory. None whatsoever.

THE PROMISE OF JESUS THAT THE CHURCH WILL SURVIVE

Indeed, we also have the promise of Jesus that the church will survive. The Lord made this promise in His response to the confession of Simon Peter; that Jesus was indeed the Christ. The Lord then said.

> And I tell you, you are Peter, and on this rock I will build my church, and the gates of Hades will not prevail against it (Matthew 16:18 NRSV).

There is the clear promise from Jesus that the church will survive. Since the Lord always keeps His promises, the church will indeed survive. There is no doubt about this.

In sum, the devil has attacked the church from both without and within. Yet his tactics will ultimately fail. The victory belongs to Jesus Christ.

SUMMARY TO QUESTION 24
HOW HAS SATAN ATTEMPTED TO DESTROY THE CHURCH?

From the very beginning of its existence, the church, the true believers in Jesus, has been the object of attack from Satan. This of course, is not surprising. We also find that he has attacked believers from both inside as well as outside of the church.

Within, the devil has attacked the church by introducing false teaching and false teachers. We find them already infiltrating the church at an early time in its history. The lying words of his ministers have lead many people astray.

Yet, God's truth is still being taught! Indeed, though false doctrine has been introduced, the truth of the gospel continues to be proclaimed.

From without, the devil has persecuted God's people. Persecution also began at an early date in the history of the church and it continues to this day. Satan attempts to destroy the church by imprisoning and killing the true believers.

Yet infiltration and persecution will not stop the work of the Lord. The church will continue to prosper because Jesus said nothing would, or could, stop its advancement. Consequently, the unstoppable ministry of Jesus Christ through His people, the church, continues.

QUESTION 25

How Will Satan Work Through The Man Of Sin?
(The Final Antichrist)

Satan will eventually have his wish and will be worshipped by human-ity. The Bible speaks of a person coming on the scene of history that will be energized by Satan and will deceive many people. He is known in Scripture by a variety of names such as "the beast," the "man of lawlessness," and the "man of sin." From Scripture, we discover many things about him. They include the following.

1. HE WILL BE ENERGIZED BY THE DEVIL

This "man of sin" will be totally energized and controlled by the devil himself. Paul wrote about this to the Thessalonians.

> The coming of the lawless one is apparent in the working of Satan, who uses all power, signs, lying wonders, and every kind of wicked deception for those who are perish-ing, because they refused to love the truth and so be saved (2 Thessalonians 2:9,10 NRSV).

The Bible says that this person does his deceptive work by the power of the devil.

2. THE ANTICHRIST

The most well-known designation of this person is that of "Antichrist." The word Antichrist is only found in the writings of the Apostle John.

John wrote.

> Children, it is the last hour. And as you have heard, "Antichrist is coming," even now many antichrists have come. We know from this that it is the last hour. . . . Who is the liar, if not the one who denies that Jesus is the Messiah? He is the antichrist, the one who denies the Father and the Son (1 John 2:18,22 HCSB).

This personage is the last of many antichrists. Among other descriptions of him, John calls antichrist a liar. His lie is that he denies the biblical truth about God the Father and God the Son.

3. THE SPIRIT OF ANTICHRIST WAS ALREADY PRESENT

In another place, John wrote that the spirit of the antichrist was already present at the time of his writing.

> But every spirit who does not confess Jesus is not from God. This is the spirit of the antichrist; you have heard that he is coming, and he is already in the world now (1 John 4:3 HCSB).

The spirit of antichrist has been with the church from the very beginning of its existence. This evil spirit continues to this day.

In 2 John, we read that antichrist is a deceiver; one who does not confess that Jesus Christ, God the Son, actually became a human being.

> Many deceivers have gone out into the world; they do not confess the coming of Jesus Christ in the flesh. This is the deceiver and the antichrist (2 John 7 HCSB).

This antichrist is described as the deceitful one.

OBSERVATIONS ON THE FINAL ANTICHRIST

From these verses we can deduce the following.

1. The spirit which characterizes the future Antichrist was at work at the time of the Apostle John.

2. A final Antichrist is expected at the end of the age.

3. The spirit of Antichrist is that of apostasy, departing from the truth.

4. The spirit of Antichrist is that of a liar, denying that Jesus is the Christ.

THE WARNING OF JESUS ABOUT ANTICHRISTS

Jesus Himself warned that false Christ's would appear and attempt to deceive the people. Matthew records Him saying the following.

> At that time if anyone says to you, 'Look, here is the Christ!' or, 'There he is!' do not believe it. For false Christs and false prophets will appear and perform great signs and miracles to deceive even the elect—if that were possible (Matthew 24:23,24 NIV).

Jesus warned about false Christs coming on the scene. We are not to believe these people or their false claims.

HE WILL CLAIM TO BE GOD

The Bible says this coming man of sin will actually claim to be God. The Apostle Paul stated this in his second letter to the Thessalonians. He wrote.

> Who opposes and exalts himself above all that is called God or that is worshiped, so that he sits as God in the temple of God, showing himself that he is God (2 Thessalonians 2:4 NKJV).

This personage will attempt to take God's rightful place as the object of worship. Indeed, he will make the arrogant claim that he is actually God! Unhappily, he will deceive people into believing that his claims are true.

THE COMPARISON OF ANTICHRIST WITH JESUS CHRIST

This final Antichrist can be compared with Jesus Christ in a number of ways.

1. ONE COMES IN HIS OWN NAME, THE OTHER IN THE NAME OF GOD THE FATHER

The Antichrist will come in his own name, while Jesus came in the name of God the Father. Jesus warned us about this.

> I have come in my Father's name, and you do not accept me; but if someone else comes in his own name, you will accept him (John 5:43 NIV).

In sum, Jesus came in the name of God the Father while this Antichrist will come in his own name, representing his father, Satan.

2. ONE IS EMPOWERED BY SATAN, THE OTHER IS EMPOWERED BY GOD THE FATHER

God the Son, Jesus Christ, was empowered by God the Father. On the other hand, Satan is the driving force behind Antichrist. The Apostle Paul said the following.

> The coming of the *lawless one* is according to the working of Satan, with all power, signs, and lying wonders (2 Thessalonians 2:9 NKJV).

Each has a different source of power, God or Satan.

3. THERE IS A FALSE TRINITY

As God by nature is a Trinity, God the Father, God the Son, and God the Holy Spirit, there will be a false trinity with Satan, the Antichrist or the beast, and the False Prophet. We are told of their demise.

> And the devil who had deceived them was thrown into the lake of fire and sulfur, where the beast and the false prophet were, and they will be tormented day and night forever and ever (Revelation 20:10 NRSV).

This unholy trinity is in contrast with the Holy Trinity.

4. ONE IS FROM ABOVE THE OTHER IS FROM BENEATH

Jesus Christ came from above. Indeed, He is God the Son who became a human being. In contrast to this, the final Antichrist is from below. Jesus made this clear when He contrasted Himself, coming from above, to the wicked religious rulers, who were coming from beneath.

> And He said to them, "You are from beneath; I am from above. You are of this world; I am not of this world" (John 8:23 NKJV).

The Lord Jesus is from above, while this man of sin, like the evil religious leaders of Jesus' day, will be from beneath.

5. ONE IS A LAMB THE OTHER IS A BEAST

Jesus Christ was a lamb, a completely harmless being. John wrote about Jesus.

> The next day John saw Jesus coming toward him, and said, "Behold! The Lamb of God who takes away the sin of the world!" (John 1:29 NKJV).

In complete contrast to this, the final Antichrist is called a beast. We read this description of him in the Book of Revelation.

And I saw a beast rising out of the sea, with ten horns and seven heads, with ten diadems on its horns and blasphemous names on its heads. And the beast that I saw was like a leopard; its feet were like a bear's, and its mouth was like a lion's mouth. And to it the dragon gave his power and his throne and great authority (Revelation 13:1,2 ESV).

The contrast between the lamb and the beast could not be more striking.

6. THERE IS GENUINE RESURRECTION VERSUS A POSSIBLE COUNTERFEIT ONE

Jesus Christ rose from the dead three days after His death on the cross. The Antichrist has a potential fake resurrection from the dead. The Bible says the following.

I saw that one of the heads of the beast seemed wounded beyond recovery—but the fatal wound was healed! All the world marveled at this miracle and followed the beast in awe (Revelation 13:3 NLT).

There is a contrast between the resurrections. One is genuine while the other is counterfeit.

7. ONE RECEIVES THE WORSHIP OF UNBELIEVERS, THE OTHER RECEIVES GODLY WORSHIP

Antichrist will receive the worship of unbelievers. Many of them will believe that he is God himself.

He was permitted to give a spirit to the image of the beast, so that the image of the beast could both speak and cause whoever would not worship the image of the beast to be killed. And he requires everyone—small and great, rich and poor, free and slave—to be given a mark on his right hand or on his forehead, (Revelation 13:15,16 HCSB).

On the other hand, Jesus Christ received the worship of believers. While each will receive worship, only One is deserving of it.

8. ONE WILL DESTROY THE OTHER

The man of sin will be destroyed at Jesus Christ's Second Coming to the earth. Paul wrote the following to the Thessalonians about this momentous event.

> And then the lawless one will be revealed, whom the Lord Jesus will overthrow with the breath of his mouth and destroy by the splendor of his coming (2 Thessalonians 2:8 NIV).

The lawless one will come to an inglorious end.

John also wrote about this event. He explained it in this manner.

> And the beast was captured, and with it the false prophet who had performed in its presence the signs by which he deceived those who had received the mark of the beast and those who worshiped its image. These two were thrown alive into the lake of fire that burns with sulfur (Revelation 19:20 NRSV).

Jesus will eventually destroy the man of sin.

In sum, the Bible says that Satan's man is coming, the man of sin, the Antichrist. While he will deceive many people, his deception will only last for a short period of time.

SUMMARY TO QUESTION 25
HOW WILL SATAN WORK THROUGH THE MAN OF SIN? (THE FINAL ANTICHRIST)

Satan has always wanted worship. He began his career by wishing to change places with God. That did not work. He will finally get his chance as he energizes a particular individual known as the "man of sin," the final Antichrist. We can make a number of important observations about this coming personage.

The Bible instructs us that this person will counterfeit Jesus Christ in a number of ways. For one thing, while Jesus came in the name of God the Father this man of sin will come in the name of Satan. Furthermore, Jesus came with the power of the living God, while this Antichrist will come in the power of Satan.

While God is by nature a Trinity, Father, Son, and Holy Spirit, Satan will have his unholy trinity, himself, the antichrist, and the false prophet. In this way, Satan will pervert God's truth.

Jesus Christ, God the Son, came from above, or heaven, while Satan's man, the final Antichrist, comes from below, or the pit. They could not be farther apart geographically.

Jesus and the man of sin are both compared to animals. Jesus is compared to a lamb while the Antichrist to a wild beast.

There is also the possibility that Antichrist will attempt to pull off a phony resurrection to counterfeit Jesus' genuine resurrection. Again, there is the desire to pervert the truth.

The worship of unbelievers is received by Antichrist while Jesus is worshipped by believers, false worship compared with true worship.

Though this man of sin will counterfeit Jesus Christ in a number of ways, he will eventually be destroyed when Christ comes again.

Therefore, Satan's man will arrive and he will deceive many people, but his rule will be short-lived.

Will God Release The Devil For A Short Time After Christ Returns?

One of the events which takes place after the Second Coming of Christ has caused a number of questions in the minds of believers. After Jesus Christ returns, He has Satan bound for a thousand years. However at the end of the thousand years, the Bible says that He releases Satan for a short period of time.

> And when the thousand years are ended, Satan will be released from his prison and will come out to deceive the nations that are at the four corners of the earth, Gog and Magog, to gather them for battle; their number is like the sand of the sea. And they marched up over the broad plain of the earth and surrounded the camp of the saints and the beloved city, but fire came down from heaven and consumed them (Revelation 20:7-9 ESV).

Why would God do something like this? Once Christ has returned and Satan has been bound, why allow him to be released for a short time and deceive the nations?

There a number of answers given to this question.

VIEW 1: HE IS ALREADY BOUND

First, there are some who believe that Satan has already been bound. They argue that his release will be immediately *before* Christ comes again, and not after the millennium; the thousand-year reign of Christ upon the earth.

Usually, those who hold this view do not believe there will be a literal one thousand year reign of Christ. Consequently, Satan is not released after the Lord returns according to this view. Therefore, this is not a real issue.

VIEW 2: HE HAS NOT BEEN BOUND

Other believers view the binding of Satan as something future. They believe that a literal millennium will occur. If this is the case, then the Bible gives us no reasons as to why this release of Satan happens.

There have been several different answers that have been offered to address this question.

THERE WILL BE SINFUL HUMANS LIVING ON THE EARTH

According to this scenario, during this period of time, the millennium, there will be sinful human beings living upon the earth. They will have non-glorified bodies. In other words, their bodies will be like the ones each of us now have.

These individuals will have been born to people who entered the millennium in similar sinful bodies. At the same time, there will those who have been changed into glorified bodies, bodies like that of the resurrected Christ. These are the believers who return with Christ to the earth, as well as other believers who have died in the past. Consequently, there will be two groups of people: those with glorified bodies and those with mortal sinful bodies.

Those who are born to people who enter the millennium, and have those sinful bodies, are not automatically guaranteed to spend eternity with the Lord. Like everyone else who has ever existed, they too must make their own personal choice to believe in the Lord.

HUMANITY HAS NO EXCUSE

Many see the release of Satan as an answer to an objection that has long been given. The excuse that is often used is as follows: if people only knew that God existed, then they would believe in Him. Indeed, this excuse has been used countless times by those who reject the idea of God's existence.

Therefore, during this last rebellion of Satan, there will be no one denying God's existence. In other words, there will be no atheists. Even though people know that God exists, and that He is a loving and caring God, some will still refuse to follow Him.

By allowing this scenario, God will once-and-for-all show humanity that rejecting Him is not based upon the fact that we cannot see Him. Even when people know that God exists, they will still reject Him. This seems to be one of the reasons why Satan is allowed to go free for a short period of time.

SIN STILL REMAINS IN THE HUMAN HEART

This further demonstrates that sin remains in the human heart apart from any influence of the devil. Not now, and not in the future, can all evil be blamed upon Satan and his evil forces. Sin is found in the human heart. The Bible says.

> The heart is devious above all else; it is perverse—who can understand it? (Jeremiah 17:9 NRSV).

Therefore, with this one last release of Satan, it becomes clear to everyone that sin can only be blamed upon those who consciously choose to sin, not Satan or anyone else. The responsibility for our sin is ultimately ours and ours alone.

In sum, if the pre-millennial scenario is correct and Satan is released after the end of a thousand year reign of Jesus Christ upon the earth, then it likely occurs to further answer the question of where sin originates. It is in the human heart.

SUMMARY TO QUESTION 26
WILL GOD RELEASE THE DEVIL FOR A SHORT TIME AFTER CHRIST RETURNS?

There is a question as to whether Satan will be released after Jesus Christ returns to the earth. Bible-believing Christians have differences of opinion on this matter.

The issue is whether there will be a one thousand year period of peace after Christ returns, a millennium. Some Christians reject the idea of a literal millennium, while others believe this is what the Scripture teaches.

Those who reject the idea of a literal millennium feel that this evil creature has already been bound in the bottomless pit. Therefore, there is no need for him to be bound again after Jesus Christ returns.

Consequently, it is not an issue since, there will be no such thing as a millennium or a thousand-year period of peace on the earth after Jesus Christ returns.

Others believe that he is yet to be bound. Those with that particular view hold that after Jesus Christ returns, there will be a one thousand year period of peace upon the earth, the millennium. At the end of this period, Satan will be released for a short time to deceive the nations.

As to why he will be released, we are not told. Therefore, whatever answer we provide is only speculation.

Some feel that it is to demonstrate, once and for all, that the rejection of the God of the Bible is ultimately one of the human heart, and not other influences. Indeed, at that time, there will be no atheists; for everyone will know that the God of the Bible exists.

However, there will be people who have to make a choice as to whether to believe in and follow this God which they know exists. His existence is not the issue. The issue will be whether or not they wish to love and serve Him. The releasing of Satan from the bottomless pit is a test for them.

Therefore, when Satan is released, those who follow him will not do so because they reject the idea of the existence of God. They know that the God of Scripture exists. Instead, they will follow this evil being because their human hearts are evil.

The fact that they will follow the devil points out a great truth. Rejection of the God of the Bible ultimately has nothing to do with whether or not we can see God with our own eyes. Rejection of God has to do with our human heart. Even when people know that a loving and caring God exists they will still find ways to reject His love and goodness.

Consequently, this may be part of the reason as to why Satan is released from the bottomless pit after being bound for one thousand years.

This briefly sums up how Bible-believers understand the passage which speaks of the binding of Satan.

QUESTION 27

What Is The Ultimate Destiny Of The Devil?

From the very start, the God of the Bible has predicted the eventual fate of the created spirit-being who became Satan, the devil. The Scripture informs us of the following.

1. SATAN'S DESTINY WAS ANNOUNCED AT HIS REBELLION

When this particular personage rebelled in heaven, his ultimate destiny was announced. We read the following account in the Book of Ezekiel.

> You traded far and wide. You learned to be violent, and you sinned. So I threw you down from God's mountain in disgrace. The guardian angel forced you out from the fiery stones. You became too proud because of your beauty. You wasted your wisdom because of your greatness. So I threw you to the ground and left you in front of the kings so that they could see you. You dishonored your own holy places because of your many sins and dishonest trade. So I set fire to you to burn you up. I turned you into ashes on the ground in the presence of all who saw you. All the nations who knew you are horrified because of you. You have come to a terrible end, and you will never exist again (Ezekiel 28:16-19 God's Word).

While this passage initially speaks of the fall of the King of Tyre, the punishments pronounced seem to go beyond this earthly king. Therefore, they are ultimately against Satan, the anointed cherub who became the devil. The destiny of the devil, therefore, was determined at the beginning.

2. IT WAS PREDICTED IN THE GARDEN OF EDEN

In the Garden of Eden, God prophesied the final destiny of Satan in the judgment He pronounced upon the serpent, the snake. We read of this in the third chapter of the Book of Genesis. It tells us the following.

> From now on, you and the woman will be enemies, and your
> offspring and her offspring will be enemies. He will crush
> your head, and you will strike his heel (Genesis 3:15 NLT).

The seed of the woman, who is Jesus Christ, will crush the head of the snake. The judgment upon the snake is ultimately a judgment upon Satan.

3. THE SERPENT WILL EAT DUST

Satan would have to eat dust. This is a prophetic picture of his final degradation. Eating dust carries with it the idea of total defeat. The prophet Micah wrote.

> They shall lick the dust like a serpent, like the crawling things
> of the earth (Micah 7:17 ESV).

There was judgment upon the snake for its part in the temptation of Adam and Eve. This judgment includes what will happen to the devil.

4. AT THE CROSS THE DEVIL WAS DEFEATED

The crushing of the serpent's head was accomplished at the cross. The Bible says the following about the victory of Jesus.

The one who commits sin is of the Devil, for the Devil has sinned from the beginning. The Son of God was revealed for this purpose: to destroy the Devil's works (1 John 3:8 HCSB).

Jesus Christ came into this world to destroy the works of the devil. The devil knows that he has been defeated. It is just a matter of time before his evil work comes to an end.

5. HE WILL BE CONFINED TO ABYSS

After Jesus Christ returns, Satan will be confined to the abyss, the bottomless pit. Scripture says the following in describing this.

Then I saw an angel coming down from heaven, holding in his hand the key to the bottomless pit and a great chain. He seized the dragon, that ancient serpent, who is the Devil and Satan, and bound him for a thousand years (Revelation 20:1,2 NRSV).

He will be confined to the abyss when the Lord Jesus returns.

6. HE WILL ULTIMATELY GO INTO THE LAKE OF FIRE

Eventually, he will spend eternity in the lake of fire. The Bible says the following somber words about his final fate.

And the devil who had deceived them was thrown into the lake of fire and sulfur, where the beast and the false prophet were, and they will be tormented day and night forever and ever (Revelation 20:10 NRSV).

This is his ultimate destination.

In fact, the Lord Jesus has said that this particular place was actually created for the devil and his angels. We read the following words.

Then he will say to those on his left, 'Depart from me, you who are cursed, into the eternal fire prepared for the devil and his angels' (Matthew 25:41 NIV).

This lake of fire will indeed be a righteous punishment for this evil being and the problems which he has caused.

7. HE WILL BE PUNISHED FOREVER

Contrary to popular belief, Satan will not be in charge in hell. There will be no organized sin with him as the leader. Everyone there will be eternally punished, including Satan.

This sums up what the Bible has to say about the final destiny of the devil. It is clear from Scripture that the Lord will eternally punish him for his horrific evil.

SUMMARY TO QUESTION 27
WHAT IS THE ULTIMATE DESTINY OF THE DEVIL?

Satan, the created being who rebelled and became the devil, has been judged in the past and he will be judged in the future. His destiny was pronounced the moment he first rebelled against God. Indeed, his fate was sealed. From Scripture, we can make the following observations.

It seems that his ultimate destiny was predicted through the judgment God pronounced upon the serpent in the Garden of Eden. The judgment announced against the serpent certainly dealt with more than a judgment on a mere animal. Like the serpent, Satan will have to eat dust. This is a sign of his judgment.

The death of Jesus Christ on the cross was, among other things, a judgment against the devil. Indeed, the Bible says that Christ came into our world to destroy the works of the devil.

When Christ returns to the earth we are told that Satan will be consigned to the bottomless pit. This is another judgment he will receive.

Satan will eventually be sent to the lake of fire. In fact, Jesus said that it was specially created as a place for his punishment, as well as for those angels who followed him. He will be punished there forever.

Therefore, this evil creature, as well as those which have followed him, will receive their rightful punishment for their rebellion against the God of Scripture.

What Is The Extent
Of Satan's Power?

It is very important to understand who our adversary the devil is, and what he is able to do. We must be careful not to attribute to him abilities and honors that belong to God and to Him alone. The Bible says the following about the limitations of the devil.

1. HE IS NOT THE OPPOSITE OF GOD

While he would like people to think so, Satan is certainly not the opposite of God. God is all-powerful, everywhere present, and all-knowing. Satan is none of these. He does not have unlimited power, he cannot be everywhere at once, and he does not know everything. He is a created, limited being. He has not always existed as an evil foe to God. In fact, he depends upon God for his very existence. It is important that we understand this.

2. HE DOES NOT KNOW THE FUTURE

The Bible makes it clear that only God knows what is going to occur in the future. The prophet Isaiah records God saying the following.

> Remember the first events, because I am God, and there is no other. I am God, and there's no one like me. From the beginning I revealed the end. From long ago I told you things that had not yet happened, saying, "My

plan will stand, and I'll do everything I intended to do" (Isaiah 46:9,10 God's Word).

Neither Satan, angels, demons, or any other created being, knows what will happen next. This is something which God alone knows.

3. HE DOES NOT KNOW WHAT WE DREAM

In addition, only someone speaking through the power of God can know what people dream. Daniel the prophet made this clear when he responded to the pagan King Nebuchadnezzar. He said the following.

> Daniel answered the king, "No wise men, enchanters, magicians, or diviners can show to the king the mystery that the king is asking, but there is a God in heaven who reveals mysteries, and he has disclosed to King Nebuchadnezzar what will happen at the end of days. Your dream and the visions of your head as you lay in bed were these" (Daniel 2:27,28 NRSV).

Note well that the wise men, magicians, enchanters could not know what the king had dreamed. Only God knows these things. Satan has no such power.

4. HE CANNOT READ OUR THOUGHTS

Because he is a created being, Satan cannot read our thoughts. He is not all-knowing like the Lord. It is God alone that knows everything; including what we think. Isaiah the prophet made the following statement about the Lord.

> Do you not know? Have you not heard? The LORD is the everlasting God, the Creator of the ends of the earth. He will not grow tired or weary, and his understanding no one can fathom (Isaiah 40:28 NIV).

None of us can begin to fathom the understanding which the God of Scripture has. He alone has this exhaustive knowledge.

In First Kings, we read the following admission of King Solomon about God knowing the thoughts of the people.

> May You hear in heaven, Your dwelling place, and may You forgive, act, and repay the man, according to all his ways, since You know his heart, for You alone know every human heart (1 Kings 8:39 HCSB).

The Lord alone knows the thoughts of people, He knows what is in our heart. No other creature in heaven or earth has this ability. Nobody.

The psalmist made this point clear when he wrote about the knowledge of the unrighteous.

They say, "The Lord does not see; the God of Jacob takes no notice."

> Take notice, you senseless ones among the people; you fools, when will you become wise? Does he who fashioned the ear not hear? Does he who formed the eye not see? Does he who disciplines nations not punish? Does he who teaches mankind lack knowledge? The Lord knows all human plans; he knows that they are futile (Psalm 94:7-11 NIV).

The Lord indeed knows our thoughts, He knows our plans, He knows everything.

We read something similar about the knowledge of the Lord in another Psalm.

> You have searched me, Lord, and you know me. You know when I sit and when I rise; you perceive my thoughts from afar. You discern my going out and my lying down; you are familiar with all my ways. Before a word is on my tongue you, Lord, know it completely. You hem me in behind and before, and you lay your hand upon me. Such knowledge is too wonderful for me, too lofty for me to attain (Psalm 139:1-6 NIV).

Only God, the Creator, has such knowledge.

Furthermore, Jesus, who is the Lord, also knew people's thoughts. We read the following in Matthew's gospel. It says.

> Knowing their thoughts, Jesus said, "Why do you entertain evil thoughts in your hearts" (Matthew 9:4 NIV).

All knowledge, or being omniscient, is an attribute of God alone.

The lack of being able to know our thoughts is another limitation in the character of Satan. It further illustrates the contrast between this created being and the Lord.

5. HE APPROACHES GOD AS A SUBORDINATE

When Satan approached God, he did not come as an equal, but rather as a subordinate. We discover this in the Book of Job.

> Now there was a day when the sons of God came to present themselves before the LORD, and Satan came also among them (Job 1:6 KJV).

It is clear that he is not an equal with the Lord. We should never treat him as such.

6. HE CANNOT TEMPT ANYONE WITHOUT GOD'S PERMISSION

We also discover that he could not tempt Job without God's permission. The Bible records the following words of the Lord to Satan.

> The LORD said to Satan, "Very well, then, everything he has is in your hands, but on the man himself do not lay a finger." Then Satan went out from the presence of the LORD (Job 1:12 NIV).

He has limited abilities. This is clear from the Scripture.

In fact, we are told that Jesus' temptation or testing from the devil was actually Spirit-led. The Bible says.

> Then Jesus was led up by the Spirit into the wilderness to be tempted by the devil (Matthew 4:1 NRSV).

Therefore, Jesus was only tested to the degree which the Holy Spirit allowed it to happen. Satan had no say so in the matter.

7. HE CANNOT INFLUENCE NATURE WITHOUT GOD'S PERMISSION

When it came to influencing nature, we also find that Satan was not able to do it without God's permission. We read the following account in the Book of Job.

> "All right, you may test him," the LORD said to Satan. "Do whatever you want with everything he possesses, but don't harm him physically." So Satan left the LORD's presence. One day when Job's sons and daughters were dining at the oldest brother's house, a messenger arrived at Job's home with this news: "Your oxen were plowing, with the donkeys feeding beside them, when the Sabeans raided us. They stole all the animals and killed all the farmhands. I am the only one who escaped to tell you." While he was still speaking, another messenger arrived with this news: "The fire of God has fallen from heaven and burned up your sheep and all the shepherds. I am the only one who escaped to tell you." While he was still speaking, a third messenger arrived with this news: "Three bands of Chaldean raiders have stolen your camels and killed your servants. I am the only one who escaped to tell you." While he was still speaking, another messenger arrived with this news: "Your sons and daughters were feasting in their oldest brother's home. Suddenly, a powerful wind swept in from the desert and hit the house on all sides. The house collapsed, and all your children are dead. I am the only one who escaped to tell you" (Job 1:12-19 NLT).

This shows that God's permission was necessary for whatever Satan wanted to do. Again, we find that he is severely limited in what he is able to do.

8. HE CANNOT PHYSICALLY HARM WITHOUT GOD'S PERMISSION

When Satan wanted to physically harm the man Job, he had to first ask God's permission. We further read in Job.

> And the Lord said to Satan, "From where have you come?" Satan answered the Lord and said, "From going to and fro on the earth, and from walking up and down on it." And the Lord said to Satan, "Have you considered my servant Job, that there is none like him on the earth, a blameless and upright man, who fears God and turns away from evil? He still holds fast his integrity, although you incited me against him to destroy him without reason." Then Satan answered the Lord and said, "Skin for skin! All that a man has he will give for his life. But stretch out your hand and touch his bone and his flesh, and he will curse you to your face (Job 2:2-5 ESV).

There is nothing he can do without the Lord allowing it. Nothing.

9. HE CANNOT KILL WITHOUT GOD'S PERMISSION

Satan cannot take a human life without first getting God's permission. Again, we read what the Lord said to him, as recorded in the Book of Job.

> And the LORD said to Satan, "Behold, he *is* in your hand, but spare his life" (Job 2:6 NKJV).

Note how the Lord limited Satan as to what he could do to Job.

The Bible does say that Satan has the power of death. We read the following in the Book of Hebrews.

Since the children have flesh and blood, he too shared in their humanity so that by his death he might break the power of him who holds the power of death—that is, the devil (Hebrews 2:14 NIV).

However this does not mean that he has the ultimate authority to cause people to die. Indeed, only God has that authority.

10. HE CANNOT TOUCH ANYTHING WITHOUT GOD'S PERMISSION

Satan cannot even touch a believer without the permission of God. Satan complained to the Lord about this.

Have you not put a hedge around him and his household and everything he has? You have blessed the work of his hands, so that his flocks and herds are spread throughout the land (Job 1:10 NIV).

God has placed a fence around each believer protecting them from the devil.

This is confirmed in a statement by the Apostle John. He wrote.

We know that anyone born of God does not continue to sin; the One who was born of God keeps them safe, and the evil one cannot harm them (1 John 5:18 NIV).

God's permission is necessary before he can touch God's people. This is so crucial for us to understand.

11. HE CANNOT FORCE BELIEVERS TO DO ANYTHING

In addition, those who have trusted in Jesus Christ have been freed from the authority of the devil. We read the following statement in the Book of Acts about what Jesus accomplished.

To open their eyes so they may turn from darkness to light, and from the power of Satan to God. Then they will receive forgiveness for their sins and be given a place among God's people, who are set apart by faith in me (Acts 26:18 NLT).

Satan therefore has no authority, no power, over the believer. None. He cannot force us to do anything against our will. Indeed, we have been set free!

11. HE IS A COWARD

In spite of all his bluster and rage, he is a coward. The Bible says.

Therefore submit to God. Resist the devil and he will flee from you (James 4:7 NKJV).

The devil can be resisted, and when he is resisted, he will leave us.

12. BELIEVERS ARE VICTORIOUS OVER SATAN BECAUSE OF CHRIST

Scripture says that believers are ultimately victorious through Jesus Christ. Paul wrote these words of triumph to the Corinthians.

But thanks be to God, who always leads us as captives in Christ's triumphal procession and uses us to spread the aroma of the knowledge of him everywhere (2 Corinthians 2:14 NIV).

Because of Jesus Christ, believers are the victors. This is the biblical truth upon which Christians must stand. Satan has been defeated.

In sum, Satan is indeed a powerful being but his power is limited. It is therefore important for us to know what he can do, as well as what he cannot do.

SUMMARY TO QUESTION 28
WHAT IS THE EXTENT OF SATAN'S POWER?

Though Satan attempts to make us think that he is the opposite of God, this is not the case. His power is limited because he is a created being, not the Creator. He lies to us when he claims some sort of equality with God.

For example, he cannot create anything. Indeed, he himself is a created being. As a created being, he is limited in what he can do.

We also discover that he cannot search the human heart or read thoughts. These characteristics belong to God and to Him alone. Satan has no such ability.

Furthermore, the devil does not know what people have dreamed. The Book of Daniel illustrates this point. Daniel, the man of God, was the only one who could tell King Nebuchadnezzar what he had dreamed. The magicians and soothsayers of Babylon could not. The devil had no such knowledge.

There is something else. The devil does not know the future. God has made it clear in His Word that He alone knows what is going to take place. Satan does not know what will occur.

We also find that the Bible says that the devil has to approach God as a subordinate. Without God's permission, he is not able to do anything. He has no power in and of himself.

For example, he cannot tempt believers unless God permits him. Therefore, any testing we receive is first approved by God because He knows the limits of what we can endure.

Moreover, he cannot, on his own, influence nature or cause any physical harm. In fact, he cannot touch anyone at all unless the Lord allows it.

Actually the devil is a coward. He is just the opposite of whom he makes himself out to be. Christians should never believe his lies. Remember that Jesus said that he is the, "Father of lies." Nothing he says should be believed.

The good news from Scripture is that believers in Jesus Christ will be ultimately victorious over Satan. Through Christ, the victory has been won. It is our responsibility to enter into the victories the Lord has provided for us.

Therefore the conflict between God and Satan is not really a struggle between two great equal and opposing powers with the outcome still in doubt. All power and authority belongs to God, and to Him alone. The victory has already been won.

Is Satan Able To
Perform Miracles?

Satan has many powers. Is the ability to perform miracles one of them? What does the Bible say about this issue? There are a number of observations that are necessary for us to make.

1. GOOD ANGELS CAN PERFORM MIRACLES

We know that good angels, through the power of God, have the ability to perform miracles. An example of this would be the blinding of the evil men at Sodom. The Bible says that the following took place.

> And they [the angels] struck with blindness the men who were at the door of the house, both small and great, so that they were unable to find the door (Genesis 19:11 NRSV).

The ability to perform miracles belongs to good angels. However, this power is given them by God Himself. They do not act on their own.

2. THE TESTIMONY OF JESUS CONCERNING GENUINE MIRACLES

When John the Baptist sent messenger to Jesus to confirm that He was the Messiah, Jesus answered as follows.

> Jesus answered John's disciples, "Go back, and tell John what you hear and see: Blind people see again, lame people are walking, those with skin diseases are made clean, deaf people

hear again, dead people are brought back to life, and poor people hear the Good News. Whoever doesn't lose his faith in me is indeed blessed" (Matthew 11:4-6 God's Word).

To demonstrate that He was the Messiah, Jesus performed miracles. John the Baptist, as well as the rest of the people, could now be certain that Jesus was whom He claimed to be; because genuine miracle-working ability belongs to God and Him alone. Satan, a created being, does not have that power.

3. SATAN PERFORMS COUNTERFEIT SIGNS

Though Satan does not have the ability to perform genuine miracles, he is able to produce counterfeit miracles or lying wonders.

Paul wrote to the Thessalonians about this idea.

> Then the man of sin will be revealed and the Lord Jesus will destroy him by what he says. When the Lord Jesus comes, his appearance will put an end to this man. The man of sin will come with the power of Satan. He will use every kind of power, including miraculous and wonderful signs. But they will be lies (2 Thessalonians 2:8,9 God's Word).

These are deceptive works. Indeed, they are not the real thing.

4. SATAN IN EGYPT DURING THE TIME OF THE EXODUS

We see Satan performing his false signs before the Exodus of the children of Israel from Egypt. The sorcerers from Egypt duplicated some of the early signs that God performed through Moses.

We read the following in the Book of Exodus.

> The Lord said to Moses and Aaron, "When Pharaoh tells you, 'Perform a miracle,' tell Aaron, 'Take your staff and throw it down before Pharaoh. It will become a serpent. '"

So Moses and Aaron went in to Pharaoh and did just as the Lord had commanded. Aaron threw down his staff before Pharaoh and his officials, and it became a serpent. But then Pharaoh called the wise men and sorcerers—the magicians of Egypt, and they also did the same thing by their occult practices (Exodus 7:8-11 HCSB).

Though these magicians were able to duplicate the miracle in some unexplained sense, it became obvious who had the real power. We then read the following words.

Each one threw down his staff, and it became a serpent. But Aaron's staff swallowed their staffs (Exodus 7:12 HCSB).

What we do know from this episode is that their power to duplicate God's signs was limited. Indeed, they could only go so far in their actions. They did not have the same ability that God gave to Moses.

In fact, by the time the third plague came upon the Egyptians, the magicians could not, in any sense, reproduce the miracle. They had to admit that it was the power of God.

The magicians tried to produce gnats using their occult practices, but they could not. The gnats remained on man and beast. "This is the finger of God," the magicians said to Pharaoh (Exodus 8:18,19 HCSB).

Therefore, the power of Satan, to counterfeit genuine miracles, is certainly limited.

5. HE HAS NO POWER OVER NATURE

We also discover that Satan needed to make a request of the Lord when he touched Job's family. He had no power over nature until the Lord allowed him to act. The Bible explains it in this manner.

The LORD said to Satan, "Very well, then, everything he has is in your hands, but on the man himself do not lay a finger." Then Satan went out from the presence of the LORD (Job 1:12 NIV).

Satan used the forces of nature against Job only after he was granted God's permission. In other words, he could not do anything in and of himself.

Therefore, anything which Satan is able to do must have God's approval. Since the devil is not God, he is not a miracle-worker. While he can perform counterfeit miracles, they are not the genuine thing.

SUMMARY TO QUESTION 29
IS SATAN ABLE TO PERFORM MIRACLES?

Satan, the created being who became the devil, is not the opposite of God. Among other things, this means that he cannot perform miracles. The only genuine miracles that have been performed have had their origin in God.

From Scripture we find that God has either directly performed miracles, or He has had them accomplished through His messengers. This includes the righteous angels, as well as certain people which He has selected.

In addition, Jesus proved that He was the genuine Messiah by the miracles He performed. In fact, He specifically referred to His miracles to support the claim that He was the long-awaited Christ. They were the testimony that He was indeed the One whom He claimed to be.

On the other hand, Satan has never performed a genuine miracle. Indeed, he has no such power.

However, since Satan is the master deceiver, he will perform phony miracles. They are done with the intent to fool people into thinking that he has certain ability which he does not possess.

We find examples of this in the story of the Exodus. Pharaoh's magicians were able to duplicate some of the early signs which Moses and Aaron performed. The Bible does not tell us how they were able to do this.

Yet we also find that there were certain signs which could not be duplicated. This is further indication that whatever powers the Lord grants to the devil, they are severely limited.

This is further confirmed in the account of Job. Satan could do nothing to affect the world of nature unless he first asked permission of the Lord. Again, we find that his power was limited.

Therefore, we are warned about the false or counterfeit signs which originate from the devil. Genuine miracles can only come from the God of the Bible.

Was The Serpent Who Spoke To Eve In The Garden Of Eden Actually Satan?

The Bible records an episode in the Book of Genesis where a serpent, or snake, actually speaks to Eve. It says.

> The snake was sneakier than any of the other wild animals that the LORD God had made. One day it came to the woman and asked, "Did God tell you not to eat fruit from any tree in the garden?" (Genesis 3:1 CEV).

Who was this personage? Was it the actual serpent speaking?

WAS IT REAL OR IMAGINARY

Many questions arise from this verse. Was this an actual serpent or some other type of creature? Was this creature real or imaginary? What is the relationship of the serpent to the devil? Did the serpent actually speak? How was the serpent able to enter the paradise of Eden when the world was made perfect?

1. IT WAS AN ACTUAL CREATURE

In Genesis three, the serpent, the snake, is an actual creature. The account is not to be understood as an allegory. This was an actual being that was with Adam and Eve in the Garden of Eden. Indeed, Scripture nowhere gives any indication for this story to be understood symbolically.

2. HOW DID SERPENT SPEAK?

If the account is not an allegory, then how can we explain the ability of a serpent to speak? The Bible provides no answer. How Eve heard the serpent is not explained either, but there is no indication that she was shocked to discover this creature could communicate with her. This has led some to speculate that before the Fall, animals had ability to speak but the Bible nowhere says this was the reality.

But it is not necessary to hold this view. In the Book of Numbers we find God speaking to the prophet Balaam through a donkey.

> Then the Lord opened the mouth of the donkey, and she said to Balaam, "What have I done to you, that you have struck me these three times" (Numbers 22:28 ESV).

Therefore, we have an example of an animal exercising human speech after the Fall. In the case of Balaam, as it seems was the case with the serpent, these are unusual events, they were not the norm.

3. THE SERPENT IS MORE SHREWD

The creature is called more "shrewd" than all other beasts. Shrewd is an ambiguous term. One the one hand, it is a virtue that the wise should cultivate. We read the following in Proverbs.

> A fool shows his annoyance at once, but a prudent man over-looks an insult (Proverbs 12:16 NIV).

In this instance, the word "prudent" means shrewd.

We also read in Proverbs.

> Every prudent man acts out of knowledge, but a fool exposes his folly (Proverbs 13:16 NIV).

As mentioned, there are negative connotations with this word, depending upon the context. Indeed, when shrewdness is misused, it becomes cunning and guile. We read about this in the Book of Job.

He frustrates the plans of the crafty, so their efforts will not succeed (Job 5:12 NLT).

The crafty can outsmart themselves.

Elsewhere in Job, we read another negative connotation of this word.

Your sin prompts your mouth; you adopt the tongue of the crafty (Job 15:5 NIV).

Therefore, the word translated shrewd can have several different meanings. Again, it all depends upon the context.

5. HE IS ALSO CUNNING

In Genesis, in stressing the craftiness of the serpent, it says he was more cunning than all other creatures the Lord had made.

The New Testament also emphasizes this fact. Paul wrote the following to the church at Corinth.

But I am afraid that just as Eve was deceived by the serpent's cunning, your minds may somehow be led astray from your sincere and pure devotion to Christ (2 Corinthians 11:3 NIV).

The New English Translation uses the word "treachery" in describing how the serpent deceived Eve in the Garden.

But I am afraid that just as the serpent deceived Eve by his treachery, your minds may be led astray from a sincere and pure devotion to Christ (2 Corinthians 11:3 NET).

By Satan's fall, the wisdom and great intellect that he had been given was perverted into an evil craftiness or treachery.

Eve, along with Adam, had been given dominion over all the creatures. However, they were tempted by Satan who was working through an inferior being.

6. THERE IS A PLAY ON WORDS IN THE HEBREW

There is something else which we would not notice in our English translations. The choice of the term *aroom* "shrewd" is one of the more obvious play on words in the Hebrew text. Indeed, the man and his wife have just been described as naked *aroam* (2:25). They will seek themselves to be shrewd (cf. 3:6) but will discover they are naked (2:25).

7. THE IDENTITY OF THE SERPENT

When we answer the question of the identity of the serpent we must answer it in a couple of ways. If all we had was the Book of Genesis, then we would not know that there was some sinister force behind the serpent and his temptation.

From the Book of Genesis, it is the serpent alone who is responsible for tempting Adam and Eve, and he alone is judged. No other beings are mentioned.

However, this is not the end of the story. Though the serpent is not explicitly identified in the Book of Genesis, or the rest of the Old Testament for that matter, he is identified with Satan in the last book of Scripture. The Bible says.

> And the great dragon was thrown down, that ancient serpent, who is called the devil and Satan, the deceiver of the whole world—he was thrown down to the earth, and his angels were thrown down with him (Revelation 12:9 ESV).

Here the serpent of old is specifically identified with the devil and Satan. Thus, at the very least, he was behind the creature which spoke to Eve in the Garden of Eden.

This identification is later restated in the Book of Revelation. We read.

> He laid hold of the dragon, that serpent of old, who is the Devil and Satan, and bound him for a thousand years (Revelation 20:2 NKJV).

The serpent is ultimately identified with the devil. This is the nature of progressive revelation. This basically means that God does not reveal everything at once. His revelation to the human race is in different parts and at different stages. Only when the final book of Scripture was being written do we have a clearer understanding of the identity of the serpent. Knowing this helps us understand what took place in Eden.

8. HE IS NOT A SUPERNATURAL BEING

It does seem clear from Scripture that there was an actual serpent in the Garden. Indeed, he is described as one of the wild animals that God had made (Genesis 1:25; 2:19). The serpent was not a supernatural being.

Yet, in some way, unknown to us, Satan used the serpent to tempt Adam and Eve. Therefore, Satan himself is the ultimate personage behind the workings of the serpent. The serpent was, therefore, the instrument the devil used to do his bidding.

9. WHY WAS HE ALLOWED TO ENTER THE GARDEN?

This brings up an important question. If the Garden of Eden was God's paradise, then why would God allow the devil, through the serpent, the right to enter this place of perfection? How did Satan gain access to Adam and Eve in the Garden of Eden through this creature which the Lord had created?

Obviously God had to allow the devil access to the Garden through the serpent. A similar situation can be found in the Book of Job where Satan had to ask God's permission to test Job. The Lord allowed Satan to tempt him, but only within certain limits. We read.

> And the Lord said to Satan, "Behold, all that he has is in your hand. Only against him do not stretch out your hand." So Satan went out from the presence of the Lord (Job 1:12 ESV).

Satan's abilities are limited to what the Lord allows. He must ask permission and he must obey the Lord. Therefore, we conclude God gave Satan the permission to allow the serpent to tempt Adam and Eve.

10. SIN IS OUR OWN DECISION

Consequently, God permitted the entrance of the serpent into the Garden for the purpose of the temptation of Adam and Eve. However, this does not mean that God wished Adam and Eve to sin, forced them to sin, or kept them unprotected from sin.

Though they were tempted by a crafty and intelligent being, they did not have to sin! God told them the consequences ahead of time and they alone made the choice to disobey Him.

Ultimately, as with every sin, it is the person's own decision. Scripture teaches that with every temptation God always provides a means to escape. The Bible says.

> But remember that the temptations that come into your life are no different from what others experience. And God is faithful. He will keep the temptation from becoming so strong that you can't stand up against it. When you are tempted, he will show you a way out so that you will not give in to it (1 Corinthians 10:13 NLT).

To sum up, blame cannot be placed upon God for the sin of Adam and Eve, for it was their own choice. In the same manner, when we sin today we cannot blame God or the devil. It is our choice.

SUMMARY TO QUESTION 30
WAS THE SERPENT WHO SPOKE TO EVE IN THE GARDEN OF EDEN ACTUALLY SATAN?

The Bible says that Eve was tempted in the Garden of Eden by a snake, a serpent. While there is every indication that the serpent was an actual animal, it was ultimately the devil which was behind the words of the snake that allowed him to tempt Eve.

We find this from a study of the totality of Scripture, not from the Book of Genesis, or from the Old Testament. Genesis does not inform us of any other personage being involved in the tempting of Adam and Eve apart from the serpent. Judgment is pronounced on the serpent alone. No other creature is punished for what the serpent did.

However, from the New Testament we find that it was Satan, the created being who became the devil, who was the personage behind the workings of the serpent.

The serpent, who was guided by the devil in some unexplained way, used his craftiness to cause Eve, and then Adam, to sin. This is how progressive revelation works. The God of the Bible does not tell humanity His truths all at once but progressively reveals them to us over time. Through progressive revelation we now know the ultimate source of the temptation of Adam and Eve, the devil himself.

Now, while God permitted Adam and Eve to be tested, He certainly did not encourage them to sin, or force them to sin. They could have resisted the temptation if they so desired. Ultimately, it was their fault for not resisting the temptation. They chose to sin.

In sum, it was Satan who was ultimately behind the speaking snake in the Garden of Eden. We learn this from the identification made in the Book of Revelation.

QUESTION 31

How Does Satan Keep Unbelievers In Spiritual Darkness?

Satan, the created spirit-being who became the devil, does not want humans to have a personal relationship with the living God. Indeed, he does all that he can to keep that from happening.

Basically this personage attempts to keep unbelievers in a state of spiritual darkness. There are a number of ways which he does this. We can make the following observation about his tactics.

1. HE WANTS PEOPLE TO DENY HIS EXISTENCE

One of the favorite ways in which Satan operates is to get people to deny that he exists. In fact, he seems to be most effective when people do not believe that there is such a creature as the devil. If he can get people to doubt or deny his existence, then he can do much of his work without their knowing it. In other words, he wants to keep them ignorant.

Indeed, as we study the Bible, we find that Satan has often approached people in disguise. For example, in the Garden of Eden he came in the form of a serpent to Adam and Eve (Genesis 3). His conversation with Eve consisted of one lie after another.

Yet his approach was crafty and ultimately convincing. She believed his lying words because he appeared to be telling the truth. Eve had no idea who it was that was tempting her to sin.

This fits what the Apostle Paul wrote to the Corinthians. He warned them that the devil appears as an angel of light.

> And it is no wonder. Even Satan tries to make himself look like an angel of light (2 Corinthians 11:14 CEV).

This unbelief which people have concerning his existence works to Satan's advantage. When people are either uniformed or misinformed about the existence of the devil, they are an easy target for him to manipulate. He comes as an angel of light when actually he is the dragon of darkness! Adam and Eve discovered this the hard way.

2. HE PREVENTS PEOPLE FROM HEARING THE GOSPEL

We know that Satan's main goal is to prevent people from hearing the good news about Jesus. The message of the New Testament is that there is forgiveness of sin offered through Jesus Christ. He sets people free from the bondage of sin. Jesus said.

> Therefore if the Son makes you free, you shall be free indeed (John 8:36 NKJV).

Satan wants to keep people bound in the slavery of sin. Therefore, the message of the gospel is hindered by the devil.

3. HE TAKES AWAY THE GOSPEL

The Bible says that the devil also takes away that which the unbeliever has heard. Jesus emphasized that in one of His parables. He said.

> The ones along the path are those who have heard; then the devil comes and takes away the word from their hearts, so that they may not believe and be saved (Luke 8:12 ESV).

Satan attempts to get the unbeliever to think about subjects or topics other than the gospel of Jesus Christ. When he does this, his goal is accomplished.

4. HE BLINDS PEOPLE TO GOD'S TRUTH

The gospel message says that there is freedom available from the power of sin. Satan attempts to blind people to that truth. Paul wrote about this to the Corinthians. He explained the tactics of the devil in this manner.

> But even if our gospel is veiled, it is veiled to those who are perishing, whose minds the god of this age has blinded, who do not believe, lest the light of the gospel of the glory of Christ, who is the image of God, should shine on them (2 Corinthians 4:3,4 NKJV).

According to this passage, the devil has placed a spiritual blindfold over the eyes of the unbelievers. He wishes to keep individuals from seeing the light of God's truth.

5. HE MISREPRESENTS THE TRUTH

There is something else which we must appreciate. Satan lies, denies, and misrepresents the truth of the living God. Indeed, in the Garden of Eden, he made the following false statement about what would take place if Adam and Eve ate the forbidden fruit. We read.

> "You will not surely die," the serpent said to the woman (Genesis 3:4 NIV).

Satan lied to Eve about what would happen to her and the man if they ate the forbidden fruit. In other words, he misrepresented the truth.

6. HE ENCOURAGES FALSE TRUST IN RELIGION

Satan also attempts to get people to falsely place their trust in things other than the message of Jesus Christ. This could mean putting their faith in themselves, religion, or good works. He wants people to feel religiously satisfied, but without having a saving knowledge of Christ. The Bible warns of doing something like this.

Sometimes what seems right is really a road to death (Proverbs 16:25 CEV).

To many people, it seems right when they go through certain religious motions or rituals. They believe that they have done their spiritual duty. Satan loves this. Indeed, he would love people to trust in some religious system rather than in the Person of Jesus Christ. Indeed, his job is accomplished when individuals have some sort of religious satisfaction apart from Jesus.

7. HE ENERGIZES HIS OWN MINISTERS

The devil is not alone in doing this. The Bible says that Satan gives power to his own ministers to do his evil work for him. Paul wrote to the Corinthians about this.

> And no wonder, for even Satan disguises himself as an angel of light. So it is no surprise if his servants, also, disguise themselves as servants of righteousness. Their end will correspond to their deeds (2 Corinthians 11:14,15 ESV).

He has his own evil ministers. Therefore, we should not be at all surprised when we see people doing devilish things which keep unbelievers in spiritual darkness.

8. HE CONTROLS PEOPLE'S HEARTS AND MINDS

Satan has the ability to control hearts and minds of people. We read about the control that he had over Judas.

> Then Satan entered into Judas called Iscariot, who was one of the twelve (Luke 22:3 NRSV).

This evil personage can exercise control over those who do not believe in Jesus. Realizing this can help us understand some of the bizarre behavior which certain people exhibit.

9. HIS GOAL IS DESTRUCTION

His ultimate goal is the destruction of people. Paul wrote about the characteristics of Satan's man, the coming Antichrist.

> Let no one deceive you in any way. For that day will not arrive until the rebellion comes and the man of lawlessness is revealed, the son of destruction (2 Thessalonians 2:4 NET).

He is the "son of destruction." This personage wants to destroy. What a contrast this is to the Lord who wants to give life!

10. THERE IS HOPE FOR ESCAPE

Fortunately, there is hope for unbelievers to escape the traps of the devil. Paul wrote the following to Timothy.

> And the Lord's slave must not engage in heated disputes but be kind toward all, an apt teacher, patient, correcting opponents with gentleness. Perhaps God will grant them repentance and then knowledge of the truth and they will come to their senses and escape the devil's trap where they are held captive to do his will (2 Timothy 2:24-26 NET).

The devil has been defeated. This is important for believers to realize. Indeed, we are battling against a foe who has already lost the war. However, he will keep on fighting until the end.

In sum, there are a number of things which the Scripture tells us about how the devil keeps people in spiritual darkness. It is important that we have some understanding of his tactics.

SUMMARY TO QUESTION 31
HOW DOES SATAN KEEP UNBELIEVERS IN SPIRITUAL DARKNESS?

The Bible says that Satan has his methods in dealing with unbelievers. These are people who do not know Jesus Christ as their Savior. The devil wants to keep these individuals in spiritual darkness. This evil personage accomplishes this in several ways. They are as follows.

First, he prevents people from believing that he actually exists. Indeed, if they don't believe in the devil, then he can easily fool them in other areas. Therefore, contrary to popular belief, he actually wants to keep people ignorant of his existence. This way he can work unnoticed.

Satan also tries to prevent people from hearing the good news about Jesus Christ. If they do not hear about the message of forgiveness from sin that Christ offers, then they cannot believe in Him. Therefore, the main goal of the devil is to keep people from believing.

When people do hear the message of Jesus Christ, Satan attempts to take away the good news once they have heard it. He does not want them to ponder the truth of the gospel. Indeed, he wants them to think about anything but the message of Jesus. He will do whatever he can to distract the person from considering God's truth.

If the devil cannot take away what the unbeliever has heard about Jesus, Satan then distorts the good news of Christ. Remember, he wants to keep them blind to the truth of the gospel.

In fact, the Bible says that there is a spiritual blindfold which Satan has put on the unbeliever. Usually he does this by misrepresenting what Jesus Christ has to offer the lost sinner.

In other words, he does everything in his power to keep people from hearing a clear intelligent presentation of the message of Christ. This is his goal.

Satan is not alone in doing this. The Bible says that he has his own ministers. He actually energizes them to do his bidding. His evil work is carried on by those who are his.

Furthermore, the devil can exercise control over people who allow him to enter into their lives. Therefore, they do his work either wittingly or unwittingly. They are basically his puppets, doing his evil deeds.

His ultimate desire is to destroy as many people as he possibly can. This is his strategy; to keep people from hearing and believing the truth about Jesus Christ.

The good news is that the Lord has provided a way out for unbelievers. If they believe in Jesus, then they can escape the traps of the devil. They can be set free!

We must understand that the devil is a defeated foe. Yet he fights and fights to keep people in spiritual darkness. It is the job of the believer to shine the light of Jesus Christ wherever we go. The light always drives out the darkness.

What Are The Methods Of The Devil Toward The Believer?

The devil attempts to lead people away from the Person of Jesus Christ. He will do whatever he can to accomplish this goal. Indeed, this evil being does not want people to believe in Christ. However, his efforts miserably fail. Millions upon millions of people trust Jesus Christ as their Savior.

While these people are now part of the family of God, this does not stop the devil from trying to lead them away from serving their Lord. Consequently, we find that Scripture warns believers in Christ that the devil attempts to keep them from being effective for the Lord.

The Bible tells us that Satan works in a number of ways toward Christians. They include the following.

1. HE TEMPTS WITH EVIL

To begin with, we find that the devil tempts God's people with evil. This is not surprising since we find that the devil tempted Jesus to disobey the commandment of the Lord. Matthew records the devil tempting Jesus with evil in the following manner.

> Again, the devil took him to a very high mountain and showed him all the kingdoms of the world and their splendor. "All this I will give you," he said, "if you will bow down

and worship me." Jesus said to him, "Away from me, Satan! For it is written: Worship the Lord your God, and serve him only" (Matthew 4:8-10 NIV).

Since only the God of the Bible is to be worshipped, it would be a sin to bow down to the devil. Jesus refused to sin.

We find that the Apostle Paul wrote to the Thessalonians about this tactic of Satan.

> That is why, when I could bear it no longer, I sent Timothy to find out whether your faith was still strong. I was afraid that the Tempter had gotten the best of you and that all our work had been useless (1 Thessalonians 3:5 NLT).

This letter was written to believers in Jesus Christ. Paul warned these Thessalonians about this work of the "Tempter." He tries to get us to do evil. This is one of his methods. We need to be aware of this.

We also need to be aware that the Lord has provided a way of escape from the various temptations we receive. Paul wrote the following words of encouragement to the Corinthians.

> No trial has overtaken you that is not faced by others. And God is faithful: He will not let you be tried beyond what you are able to bear, but with the trial will also provide a way out so that you may be able to endure it (1 Corinthians 10:13 NET).

Believers will indeed be tempted. However, the Lord always provides a way of escape from that temptation.

2. HE INSPIRES WICKED THOUGHTS

The Bible also teaches us that Satan inspires evil thoughts. We find an example of this in the Book of Acts. Scripture records the sin of a married couple named Ananias and Sapphira. Peter said to this man Ananias that Satan had caused him to lie to the Holy Spirit.

Then Peter said, "Ananias, how is it that Satan has so filled your heart that you have lied to the Holy Spirit and have kept for yourself some of the money you received for the land" (Acts 5:3 HCSB).

Notice that it was Satan who filled the heart of this believer to lie. Ananias had to take the time to think about how he was going to lie to the Christians. These evil thoughts of his were inspired by Satan. Unfortunately, Ananias acted upon them.

This is the opposite of the things which the Lord wants us to think about. Paul wrote the following to the Philippians about what our thoughts should be centered upon.

Finally, brothers and sisters, keep your thoughts on whatever is right or deserves praise: things that are true, honorable, fair, pure, acceptable, or commendable (Philippians 4:8 God's Word).

The New Living Translation puts it this way.

And now, dear brothers and sisters, let me say one more thing as I close this letter. Fix your thoughts on what is true and honorable and right. Think about things that are pure and lovely and admirable. Think about things that are excellent and worthy of praise (Philippians 4:8 NLT).

While Satan is able to place wicked thoughts into the minds of believers, the Lord wants us to think on godly things. Ultimately, it is we, and we alone, who make the choice as to which thoughts our minds will dwell upon. We can choose to think godly thoughts, or evil thoughts.

3. HE OPPOSES THOSE WHO ARE IN GOD'S SERVICE

The devil is opposed to everything which is good. However, he is particularly interested in opposing those who are in service to the Lord. Paul testified that Satan hindered him from coming to Thessalonica.

Because we wanted to come to you—I, Paul, again and again—but Satan hindered us (1 Thessalonians 2:18 ESV).

In this instance, this evil being tried to stop the work of God by keeping Paul from visiting the church. His tactics are still the same today. Indeed, he does what he can to keep the work of the Lord from going forward.

4. HE MAKES ACCUSATIONS AGAINST GOD'S PEOPLE

Satan also makes accusations against the people of God. We read the following in the Book of Zechariah.

Then he showed me Joshua the high priest standing before the Angel of the Lord, with Satan standing at his right side to accuse him (Zechariah 3:1 HCSB).

Here we find that the devil is an accuser of the people of the Lord.

This truth is further developed in the New Testament. Indeed, we find that God's people are constantly accused by this evil being. We read of this in the Book of Revelation. It says.

Then I heard a loud voice shouting across the heavens, "It has happened at last—the salvation and power and kingdom of our God, and the authority of his Christ! For the Accuser has been thrown down to earth—the one who accused our brothers and sisters before our God day and night" (Revelation 12:10 NLT).

The devil is constantly making accusations against God's people. Fortunately, believers have Jesus Christ as our Advocate with God the Father. He speaks on our behalf, answering these accusations of the evil one.

5. HE INTIMIDATES GOD'S PEOPLE

Another one of Satan's tactics is intimidation. He wants to intimidate God's people from doing what they know is right. In fact, Satan is compared to a roaring lion which is constantly on the prowl. Peter wrote.

> Be alert and of sober mind. Your enemy the devil prowls around like a roaring lion looking for someone to devour (1 Peter 5:8 NIV).

We are commanded to be alert to this bullying. Therefore, we should not be intimidated by this evil creature who is constantly attempting to devour us. Jesus Christ has been victorious over the devil. He is constantly watching over us. We should never forget this!

6. HE SEDUCES BELIEVERS TO SIN

Satan by his craftiness can seduce believers to sin. Paul emphasized this when he wrote to the Corinthians. He said.

> But I am afraid that as the serpent deceived Eve by its cunning, your thoughts will be led astray from a sincere and pure devotion to Christ (2 Corinthians 11:3 NRSV).

We all have our weaknesses. The devil knows our particular weaknesses and attempts to exploit them. Therefore, we must be constantly on guard against this tactic.

7. HE DIVERTS FROM GOD'S TRUTH

Satan tries to turn the minds of believers to the temporal things, not the eternal. Paul encourages believers to set their minds on things eternal. He wrote the following words to the Corinthians about thinking about things that will last forever.

For our present troubles are quite small and won't last very long. Yet they produce for us an immeasurably great glory that will last forever! So we don't look at the troubles we can see right now; rather, we look forward to what we have not yet seen. For the troubles we see will soon be over, but the joys to come will last forever (2 Corinthians 4:17,18 NLT).

One of the methods of the devil is to divert people from the truth of the Lord. If he can get us to think of meaningless things that take place in this world then he is accomplishing his task.

8. HE GETS BELIEVERS TO COMPROMISE

The Bible says that Satan attempts to get believers in Christ to compromise their convictions. This is something which we should never do. Indeed, Jesus made it clear that we can only have one master. He said the following words in the Sermon on the Mount.

No one can serve two masters; for a slave will either hate the one and love the other, or be devoted to the one and despise the other. You cannot serve God and wealth (Matthew 6:24 NRSV).

The enemy wants believers to compromise the things of God. Indeed, he does not want us to take a stand for the things which are righteous.

9. HE PLACES DOUBT IN THE MINDS OF BELIEVERS

Satan places doubt in the minds of those who believe in the God of the Bible. In fact, this has been his tactic from the very beginning. In the Book of Genesis, we read of the doubts which he placed in the mind of the woman Eve.

Now the serpent was the most cunning of all the wild animals that the LORD God had made. He said to the woman, "Did God really say, 'You can't eat from any tree in the garden?'" (Genesis 3:1 HCSB).

Doubts will hinder believers from being effective in the Lord's service. It will keep us from following the Lord in the manner in which we should. We must remember that it is Satan which puts doubts in our mind about the goodness of God.

10. HE WANTS BELIEVERS IN SPIRITUAL DARKNESS

Satan attempts to get the believer to feel separated from God. He wants to cause believers to be a state of spiritual darkness. Believers can indeed stray away from the Lord and find themselves in a darkened state.

However, when a person trusts the Lord, they are able to walk in the light. We do not have to walk in the darkness. Jesus Christ has conquered the darkness!

In the Old Testament, we read of what the Lord said to those who are living their lives in darkness.

> Who among you fears the LORD and obeys his servant? If
> you are walking in darkness, without a ray of light, trust in
> the LORD and rely on your God (Isaiah 50:10 NLT).

Those in darkness are to trust in the Lord, to walk in the light. This is always possible for the believer in Jesus Christ, no matter how dark their life has become. Simply stated, the Lord wants people in light while Satan wants them in darkness.

11. HE ASSAULTS BELIEVERS WITH UNFOUNDED CRITICISM

Believers can be the beneficiary of unfounded criticism. This is ultimately the work of the devil, as the Old Testament character Job found out. After he went through all of his terrible suffering, which included losing family, wealth, and physical health, he was told the following by one of his "friends."

> Your words have steadied the one who was stumbling, and
> braced the knees that were buckling. But now that this has

happened to you, you have become exhausted. It strikes you, and you are dismayed. Isn't your piety your confidence, and the integrity of your life your hope? Consider: who has perished when he was innocent? Where have the honest been destroyed? (Job 4:7-8 HCSB).

His friend assumed his sufferings were a result of some sin in his life. This was not the case. His criticism of Job was unfounded.

This is an important lesson for each of us to learn. Hardship and disasters for the Christian does not necessarily mean that there is sin in their life. God may be doing something for reasons which we do not understand. We must always allow for that possibility when we think of criticizing someone for things that are beyond their control.

In sum, we find that there are many ways in which the devil deals with those who believe in Jesus Christ. It is essential that each believer be aware of these methods. Indeed, once we know how he works we can constantly be on guard against his evil ways.

SUMMARY TO QUESTION 32
WHAT ARE THE METHODS OF THE DEVIL TOWARD THE BELIEVER?

The devil does not want anyone to follow Jesus Christ. However, millions of people do trust the Lord as their Savior. While the devil has lost these people, this does not stop him from trying to influence Christians in a negative way. The Bible warns us of this. Consequently, there are a number of things that Satan does to the believer in an attempt to get them off the straight and narrow.

For one thing, he tempts believers to do evil. While Satan tempts us, the Lord always provides a way of escape. This is a promise of God. Indeed, we do not have to sin!

Satan also inspires wicked thoughts. The devil does not want us to trust the Lord so he plants thoughts in the mind of believers to do evil.

Again, through the power of the Holy Spirit, we can resist these evil thoughts.

Satan is also in direct opposition to those who are in God's service. He does what he can to hinder us who are attempting to fulfill God's ministry. However, through the power and authority of Jesus Christ we can always thwart his opposition.

The devil also makes accusations against God's people. We are told that he accuses us day and night before the Lord. Fortunately, we have Jesus Christ pleading the case for us. Indeed, He is our Advocate.

Satan also intimidates Gods' people. This evil personage wants to keep Christians from doing that which they know is right. Often he does this by frightening believers. However, the Bible says we should not fear Satan for he can only do that which God allows him to do.

The Bible says Satan seduces believers to sin and divert them from God's truth. He knows our weaknesses and tries to exploit them. Since each of us have our weaknesses, we need to be aware of them, and to be on guard against temptations in this area.

This evil being also causes doubts in the minds of believers. The devil wants us to question whether or not God has really spoken. In other words, he denies God's Word. This has been his tactic from the very beginning.

The devil also attempts to keep us in spiritual darkness. He does not want us to walk in the light of the Lord. On the other hand, those who trust in the Lord are called the "children of light." We need to live our lives in that light.

The devil also assaults believers with unfounded criticism. Believers often suffer because Satan inspires people to say evil things about them which are not true. We must realize that this is something which takes place. While we cannot stop others from saying things about us, we can certainly not be the ones who gossip about others. Indeed, we do not ever want to be guilty of criticizing another brother or sister when we do not know the facts.

Believers should not be ignorant of these devices. In fact, these methods of the devil have been the same from the beginning. Fortunately, the Bible warns us ahead of time about these tactics. In this way, we can be prepared for them when they do come upon us. Furthermore, we must realize that we are able to resist them through the power of the Lord.

QUESTION 33

Can Satan Cause Physical Harm To Believers?

While Satan does not have the power to work miracles, and has no power over nature, he can employ physical forces against believers, if God allows it. These forces can cause harm to the believer; both physically and emotionally. Scripture provides three examples of this occurring. They are as follows.

1. THE STORY OF JOB

We find five different examples in the life of Job of Satan being able to touch a believer. Scripture tells us that God allowed Satan to cause both physical and emotional harm to this man of God. The Bible records the following.

> A messenger arrived at Job's home with this news: "Your oxen were plowing, with the donkeys feeding beside them, when the Sabeans raided us. They stole all the animals and killed all the farmhands. I am the only one who escaped to tell you." While he was still speaking, another messenger arrived with this news: "The fire of God has fallen from heaven and burned up your sheep and all the shepherds. I am the only one who escaped to tell you." While he was still speaking, a third messenger arrived with this news: "Three bands of Chaldean raiders have stolen your camels and killed your servants. I am the only one who escaped to tell you."

While he was still speaking, another messenger arrived with this news: "Your sons and daughters were feasting in their oldest brother's home. Suddenly, a powerful wind swept in from the desert and hit the house on all sides. The house collapsed, and all your children are dead. I am the only one who escaped to tell you" (Job 1:14-19 NLT).

His children were killed, his property was destroyed, his livelihood was stolen, and his servants were killed. Scripture tells us that Satan was behind each of these losses (Job 1:1-13). After these things, Job suffered physically with painful boils. The Bible says.

So Satan went out from the presence of the LORD, and inflicted loathsome sores on Job from the sole of his foot to the crown of his head (Job 2:7 NRSV).

Consequently, we find that God allowed Satan, within certain limits, to bring these problems to this man Job.

2. THE WOMAN WITH THE INFIRMITY

Another such case is found in the New Testament. There was a woman whom Jesus healed of a difficult physical ailment. We read the following in the Gospel of Luke about this episode.

And just then there appeared a woman with a spirit that had crippled her for eighteen years. She was bent over and was quite unable to stand up straight (Luke 13:11 NRSV).

We are told that a particular "spirit" had crippled here for many years to the place where she could not stand up straight.

The religious leaders were upset because Jesus was about to heal her on the Sabbath. This was the one day of the week, the day of rest, that God had commanded His people to observe.

Jesus then explained why He was going to heal her on the Sabbath day. We discover that He was actually going to free her from the bondage of Satan. He explained it in this manner.

> Then should not this woman, a daughter of Abraham, whom Satan has kept bound for eighteen long years, be set free on the Sabbath day from what bound her? (Luke 13:16 NIV).

This woman, who is called a daughter of Abraham, was attending a place of worship. Scripture indicates that she was a believer, not someone demon-possessed.

Consequently, there is nothing in this account which suggests that she was an evil person, or someone engaged in immorality. She was a believer who had a physical problem that had an evil origin.

Jesus came to set her, as well as others like her, free from this bondage. The Bible says of His ministry.

> God anointed Jesus of Nazareth with the Holy Spirit and with power, who went about doing good and healing all who were oppressed by the devil, for God was with Him (Acts 10:38 NKJV).

Jesus sets people free from the powers of darkness. This episode is a prime example of this taking place.

3. PAUL'S THORN IN THE FLESH

Finally, we have the case of the Apostle Paul. He had what he called a "thorn in the flesh." We find him writing the following words about this to the Corinthians.

> So to keep me from becoming conceited because of the surpassing greatness of the revelations, a thorn was given me in the flesh, a messenger of Satan to harass me, to keep me from becoming conceited. Three times I pleaded with the Lord

about this, that it should leave me. But he said to me, "My grace is sufficient for you, for my power is made perfect in weakness." Therefore I will boast all the more gladly of my weaknesses, so that the power of Christ may rest upon me (2 Corinthians 12:7-9 ESV).

The "thorn in the flesh" was some type of unexplained physical ailment. We must not overlook the origin of the "thorn in the flesh." Paul called it a "messenger of Satan" We also note that three times he asked the Lord to take it away. Each time God said no.

WE CAN OVERCOME ALL PROBLEMS THROUGH JESUS CHRIST

The Bible promises that God, through Jesus Christ, will provide a way to endure any testing that a believer may experience. We read the following in First Corinthians.

No temptation has overtaken you except what is common to humanity. God is faithful and He will not allow you to be tempted beyond what you are able, but with the temptation He will also provide a way of escape, so that you are able to bear it (1 Corinthians 10:13 HCSB).

No testing will be beyond the ability of the believer to cope. God will always provide a remedy for our problems.

GOD'S GLORY WAS THE RESULT

As was the case in all three instances, each situation ultimately resulted in God being glorified. While we might not understand why we go through these times of physical and emotional distress, believers can be confident that God has a plan behind all of it.

Ultimately it will glorify Himself and further His program for this world. Of this, we can be assured of.

SUMMARY TO QUESTION 33
CAN SATAN CAUSE PHYSICAL HARM TO BELIEVERS?

It is possible for Satan to inflict physical harm on believers. The Bible gives us a number of examples of this. However, this is always done with the permission of the Lord. We can make the following observations.

From the biblical account of Job, we find that Satan was able to cause harm to this man Job, but only under certain strict limits. Satan could not do whatever he wanted to with him. In other words, the devil could only do what the Lord allowed him to do. Nothing else.

In the gospel of Luke we have an account of Jesus healing a woman with a certain physical infirmity. In doing so, He testified that Satan had bound this woman with this sickness for some eighteen years.

In fact, there is no indication whatsoever that her illness was a result of some sin in her life. God had an unstated purpose in allowing Satan to place her in such a condition.

This is something which we too must recognize when we, or others, have similar ailments. Indeed, God may have a purpose in the sickness which is completely unknown to us. This is why we must always trust Him; even when we do not understand everything that is taking place.

In another incident, the Apostle Paul seemingly had a physical illness which he termed as a "messenger from Satan." Like the previous two examples, there is no indication that this occurred because there was some sin in his life.

Furthermore, the Lord would not remove this problem from him. Instead, the Lord told Paul that His grace was sufficient.

Therefore, we find that God, at times, does allow Satan to physically harm believers. As we have stressed, it is always within certain limits.

Furthermore, God will never test believers beyond what they can endure. Never! Indeed, the Lord has promised to always provide a way out from the testing. This is a promise in which we can always trust!

QUESTION 34

When Does Satan Spiritually Attack The Believer?

While the devil may attack the believer in Jesus Christ at any time, he will always do it when he thinks it is to his advantage. We see this method, time and time again, in the Scriptures. There are a number of things we can learn from Scripture as to when and how he will attack.

1. HE OFTEN ATTACKS AFTER A GREAT SPIRITUAL EXPERIENCE

Satan will tempt believers after they have had a successful spiritual experience. Indeed, we find that Satan attacked Jesus right after His baptism. The Bible says.

> Then John gave in to him. After Jesus was baptized, he immediately came up from the water. Suddenly, the heavens were opened, and he saw the Spirit of God coming down as a dove to him. Then a voice from heaven said, "This is my Son, whom I love—my Son with whom I am pleased . . . Then the Spirit led Jesus into the desert to be tempted by the devil (Matthew 3:16,17; 4:1 God's Word).

This should teach us a lesson. After a great spiritual experience we should be ready for spiritual attacks from the enemy. He wants to bring us down from our spiritual high.

2. HE ATTACKS AT THE BEGINNING OF A NEW SPIRITUAL ENDEAVOR

Satan also will attack when someone is beginning a new spiritual quest. We discover that right after Jesus was attacked by the devil, He began His public ministry. The Bible says.

> From then on Jesus began to preach, "Repent, because the kingdom of heaven has come near" (Matthew 4:17 HCSB).

Knowing that Jesus was about to begin His ministry to the world, Satan attacked Him.

3. WHEN BELIEVERS ARE PHYSICALLY VULNERABLE

We also find Satan coming when believers are in a weak position. This can be either physically or emotionally. The Bible says that Jesus was attacked after He had fasted for forty days.

> After He had fasted 40 days and 40 nights, He was hungry. Then the tempter approached Him and said, "If You are the Son of God, tell these stones to become bread" (Matthew 4:2,3 HCSB).

Obviously Jesus was in a weakened physical condition when Satan confronted Him. The enemy often comes at a time when we are at our weakest.

4. WHEN A BELIEVER IS ALONE

We also find Satan attacking when people are alone. The Bible says that Satan chose to tempt Jesus when He was alone. Matthew writes.

> Then Jesus was led up by the Spirit into the wilderness to be tempted by the devil (Matthew 4:1 NRSV).

When no other human being is there to reach out to, the enemy comes to tempt. This is something else we must always realize.

5. FROM AN UNEXPECTED SOURCE

Often times Satan will attack us from an unexpected source. In other words, it comes by way of someone from whom we would least expect.

After Jesus had told His disciples that He was going to Jerusalem to die and then be raised the third day, He was rebuked from an unexpected source. The Bible explains what happened in this manner.

> And Peter took him aside and began to rebuke him, saying, "God forbid it, Lord! This must never happen to you." But he turned and said to Peter, "Get behind me, Satan! You are a stumbling block to me; for you are setting your mind not on divine things but on human things" (Matthew 16:22-23 NRSV).

This is an unfortunate occurrence, but it happens much too often. Satan comes to the believer through the sin of another believer. These are the attacks that hurt the most.

6. HE ALWAYS COMES BACK AND ATTACKS AGAIN

After Satan attacks a believer and then leaves, we can rest assured that he will always return again. We read the following in Luke about what took place after Jesus' temptation.

> When the devil had finished every test, he departed from him until an opportune time (Luke 4:13 NRSV).

Though the believer may win a temporary victory over the devil in their spiritual battle, Satan will return to fight at another time. This is something we can be certain of.

While Satan does attack, and sometimes entices believers to fall into sin, ultimately we are victorious through Jesus Christ. This is the promise of God! The Apostle Paul declared.

The Lord will rescue me from every evil work and will bring me safely into His heavenly kingdom. To Him be the glory forever and ever! Amen (2 Timothy 4:18 HCSB).

Again we stress, the victory belongs to the Lord. Let us always remember this.

SUMMARY TO QUESTION 34
WHEN DOES SATAN SPIRITUALLY ATTACK THE BELIEVER?

We should be well-aware of the various ways in which Satan works. We know that he attacks believers when he thinks it will be to his advantage. We can make the following observations about this.

Satan likes to attack believers in Christ after a great spiritual experience. This is nothing new. Indeed, it was after Jesus' baptism, when He was first publicly shown to be God the Son, that Satan tempted Jesus for forty days. We should expect the same type of attacks to happen to us after we have had a victorious experience.

The devil also attacks right before someone is about to begin a new spiritual venture. We also learn this lesson from Jesus' temptation. It was immediately before Jesus began His public ministry that the devil attacked Him.

We learn a further lesson from Jesus' temptation. Satan attacks people when they are physically vulnerable. The gospels tell us that the devil tempted Jesus after the Lord had fasted for some forty days. Obviously He was physically spent. We should expect the same type of attacks on us when we are in a vulnerable state.

Satan also likes to attack believers when they are alone. Jesus was by Himself during the forty-day period of temptation by Satan. During that entire time, there was no human to which He could call upon for help. This same type of temptation will also happen to us when we are alone.

There are times when Christians will be attacked from an unexpected source. In fact, we find that Jesus rebuked His own apostle, Peter, for allowing Satan to speak through him. Again, we should expect spiritual attacks to also come in this way.

We must also realize that Satan will never go away. He may leave for a while but he will attack again. Christians, therefore, must always be on guard against these attacks. The good news is that we can be rescued from these attacks by the power of the Holy Spirit. Victory is the Lord's!

QUESTION 35

Can Believers Be The Unwitting Tools Of Satan?

Though believers have trusted Jesus Christ as their Savior, and have committed their lives to Him, they can actually become unwitting tools of Satan. The Bible provides some examples of this unfortunate occurrence.

DAVID NUMBERING ISRAEL

The Bible gives the account of King David numbering the people of Israel. It explains what took place in the following manner.

> Satan stood up against Israel and incited David to count the people of Israel (1 Chronicles 21:1 HCSB).

While many translations use the proper name "Satan" to illustrate who was behind this event, it is possible that a human adversary was involved. For example, the New English Translation reads this way.

> An adversary opposed Israel, inciting David to count how many warriors Israel had (1 Chronicles 21:1 NET).

Satan, or a human adversary, was the motivating force behind David numbering the people of Israel. David's sin caused God's judgment against the nation.

Interestingly, we find that the ultimate permission for David to number the people of Israel came from the Lord. The Bible says.

> Again the anger of the LORD was aroused against Israel, and He moved David against them to say, "Go, number Israel and Judah" (2 Samuel 24:1 NKJV).

Again, Satan, or some human adversary, could not incite David unless he was given permission by the Lord. Yet David chose to be a tool of Satan in his numbering of Israel.

PETER AND JESUS

We also have the account of Jesus rebuking Peter and calling him "Satan." Matthew records the following incident.

> So Peter took him aside and began to rebuke him: "God forbid, Lord! This must not happen to you!" But he turned and said to Peter, "Get behind me, Satan! You are a stumbling block to me, because you are not setting your mind on God's interests, but on man's" (Matthew 16:22,23 NET).

When Peter attempted to get Jesus to bypass the cross, he was speaking as an instrument of the devil. Jesus addressed him in that manner.

Therefore, sad as it is to admit, believers can be an unwitting tool of the enemy. Realizing this, we should be motivated not to allow ourselves to be put in a position where the devil is, in fact, using us. Consequently, we should constantly be on guard.

SUMMARY TO QUESTION 35
CAN BELIEVERS BE THE UNWITTING TOOLS OF SATAN?

Believers in Jesus Christ are children of the living God. We are part of His family. Unfortunately, Christians can unwittingly become tools of the devil. Scripture gives various accounts where their actions were satanically led.

We discover this with the case of King David numbering the people of Israel. It was Satan, or possibly a human adversary, which motivated David to do this. Whatever the case may be, he became a tool of the evil one by doing this.

Furthermore, we are told that the Lord allowed this to happen. Therefore, David, incited by the devil, numbered the people of Israel. While God did not desire this to happen, He did allow it.

When Simon Peter rebuked Jesus for speaking about going to Jerusalem and dying on the cross, it was Satan speaking through this disciple. Jesus, in turn, rebuked Peter for such words. If Peter, the great apostle, can be an instrument of the devil at some time, then certainly the same holds true for any of us. We too can be used by devil if we are not being led by the Holy Spirit.

Therefore, believers can come under satanic influence, and do things that are contrary to God's will and His plan. This should cause us to seek to be controlled by the Holy Spirit at all times so that we don't become the devil's instrument.

QUESTION 36

How Can The Believer Have Victory
Over The Devil? (Ephesians 6:12-18)

While the Bible presents the devil as a powerful and cunning oppo-
nent, it also tells us that Christians can have victory over this enemy.
John wrote.

> You are from God, little children, and you have conquered
> them, because the One who is in you is greater than the one
> who is in the world (1 John 4:4 HCSB).

Note that the One who is in us, Jesus, is greater than anyone who is in
this world. This includes the devil.

John also wrote about how God securely holds those who believe in
Him. He explained it in this manner.

> We know that those who have become part of God's fam-
> ily do not make a practice of sinning, for God's Son holds
> them securely, and the evil one cannot get his hands on them
> (1 John 5:18 NLT).

Since we are in His hand, the evil one cannot get his hands on us. This
is indeed a comforting thought.

THINGS WE MUST REMEMBER ABOUT THE BELIEVER AND SIN

There are a couple of important points we must remember about the
believer and sin. They include the following.

1. IT IS OUR OWN CHOICE WHETHER OR NOT WE SIN

It must be emphasized that Satan cannot make the believer do anything! The Bible says that when a Christian sins, it is because he or she has chosen to sin. Indeed, it is not the responsibility of anyone else. Satan can entice someone to sin, but he cannot force them to sin. We make that choice ourselves.

2. WE ARE IN JESUS CHRIST: SATAN CANNOT HARM US

There is another thing which is important for us to realize. Satan cannot recapture that person who is "in Christ." Therefore, Satan is a defeated enemy, one who ultimately will be thrown into the lake of fire. However, until that time, he is still very active in our world. Consequently the believer must take the proper steps to win victory over this enemy.

3. WE WILL HAVE SOME VICTORIES AND SOME DEFEATS

While believers are living in this world-system, and battling the attacks of the devil, it is possible to achieve temporary victories over this foe. These victories can only come through faith in Jesus Christ. While victory is always possible, occasional defeat will occur, if the believer fails to do their part.

Though these defeats do not affect the final outcome, they can hinder a person's Christian testimony, as well as their spiritual growth. Therefore, we need to discover how victory over the devil can be achieved.

THERE ARE STEPS TO TAKE

The following are some steps that the believer in Jesus Christ should take to win the spiritual battle against the enemy.

1. WE MUST UNDERSTAND OUR ENEMY

It is important that we understand our enemy. We need to know what he is able to do, his limitations, and the various ways in which he works. The Bible encourages us to do the following.

Put on the full armor of God so that you can stand against the tactics of the Devil (Ephesians 6:11 HCSB).

Knowing how to put on our Christian armor can only be discovered from a study of God's Word. Satan takes advantage of those who are spiritually immature and ignorant.

2. WE NEED TO KNOW HIS METHODS

We also need to know how the devil works. Indeed, we are not to be ignorant of his methods. The Bible says the following.

And we do this so that we may not be outwitted by Satan; for we are not ignorant of his designs (2 Corinthians 2:11 NRSV).

It is important to know his methods if we are going to win spiritual victories.

3. WE MUST PERSONALLY TEST THE SPIRITS

Believers have a responsibility to personally test the various spirits. John wrote the following to the believers in his day.

Dear friends, do not believe every spirit, but test the spirits to determine if they are from God, because many false prophets have gone out into the world (1 John 4:1 HCSB).

This is something we must actively do, we are not to sit by passively. Indeed, we are to test the spirits because not everything which claims to come from God is from God.

4. WE NEED TO BE ACTIVELY WATCHING

The Bible tells us to be watching for these tricks of the devil. Peter wrote the following to the believers.

Be sober! Be on the alert! Your adversary the Devil is prowling around like a roaring lion, looking for anyone he can devour (1 Peter 5:8 HCSB).

We should be on guard against his attacks at all times. This is especially true since we are told that he is constantly on the prowl.

5. WE MUST RESIST HIM WHEN HE COMES

The Bible tells believers to resist the devil. James wrote the following word of instruction to the believers.

> Therefore submit to God. Resist the devil and he will flee from you (James 4:7 NKJV).

Resist has the idea of "withstand," or to "stand our ground." By standing our ground, Satan can be overcome.

John wrote to believers about winning the spiritual battle with Satan. He put it this way.

> I am writing to you who are mature because you know Christ, the one who is from the beginning. I am writing to you who are young because you have won your battle with Satan (1 John 2:13 NLT).

Note that even the young, or new believers, have won the battle with Satan.

6. WE NEED TO REALIZE OUR WEAK AREAS

Every human being has areas in their life in which they are vulnerable. Satan knows these areas. Consequently believers should be especially alert from attacks in the areas where they are the weakest.

Therefore, we find that the Bible commands us not to give any opportunity for the devil to work. Paul wrote.

> And do not make room for the devil (Ephesians 4:27 NRSV).

It is important to know the areas in which we are personally weak. We must admit these weaknesses and be on the guard against attacks in these particular areas.

7. THE BATTLE IS NOT IN OUR STRENGTH

We learn a valuable lesson from Michael the archangel in his dealing with Satan. We read the following in the Book of Jude.

> But when the archangel Michael contended with the devil and disputed about the body of Moses, he did not dare to bring a condemnation of slander against him, but said, "The Lord rebuke you!" (Jude 9 NRSV).

From the example of Michael we learn that we should not personally defy the devil. We need to respect his power. Therefore, we should neither underestimate nor overestimate him.

8. WE MUST AVOID THE SITUATION

As much as is humanly possible, believers should avoid any situation that can cause us to sin. Consequently, we should separate ourselves from the source of the temptation. Paul wrote.

> Keep away from every kind of evil (1 Thessalonians 5:22 NLT).

By separating ourselves from a particular sin, both morally and geographically, a temporary victory can be won.

However, all victories are only temporary because temptation will always come as long as we are in these sinful bodies.

9. WE NEED TO PUT ON THE FULL ARMOR OF GOD

The believer has authority over the unseen realm by putting on the spiritual armor that God has provided. Paul wrote the following.

> For our battle is not against flesh and blood, but against the rulers, against the authorities, against the world powers of this darkness, against the spiritual forces of evil in the heavens. This is why you must take up the full armor of God, so that you may be able to resist in the evil day, and having prepared everything, to take your stand (Ephesians 6:12,13 HCSB).

The armor consists of spiritual realities that believers need to appropriate every day. By daily surrendering ourselves to the Lord, and placing our faith in Him, we can take advantage of these spiritual realities, because it is a spiritual battle in which we are fighting. The Bible says.

> For the weapons of our warfare are not merely human, but they have divine power to destroy strongholds. We destroy arguments (2 Corinthians 10:4 NRSV).

These spiritual realities are compared to the outfit a Roman soldier would wear. Our armor consists of the following.

THE BELT OF TRUTH

One of our weapons of warfare in the spiritual realm is the belt of truth. Paul wrote.

> Stand your ground, putting on the sturdy belt of truth and the body armor of God's righteousness (Ephesians 6:14 NLT).

The belt of truth refers to the truth of the Word of God as well as the truthfulness we should display in our daily lives. Since Satan is always a liar, we need to concern ourselves with the truth and nothing but the truth.

THE BREASTPLATE OR ARMOR OF RIGHTEOUSNESS

We are told to put on the breastplate, or armor, of righteousness. Paul wrote.

Stand, therefore, with . . . righteousness like armor on your chest (Ephesians 6:14 HCSB).

This refers to doing the right thing. We can only do the right thing after we have put on the righteousness of Jesus Christ. This happens when a person trusts Christ as Savior.

Paul wrote to the Romans about our present position in Jesus Christ. He said.

Therefore being justified by faith, we have peace with God through our Lord Jesus Christ (Romans 5:1 KJV).

Believers are at peace with God because of what Jesus Christ has done on our behalf.

SHOES TO SPREAD THE GOOD NEWS

Believers are now able to do that which is right in the sight of the Lord. Our feet also need to be covered by God's armor. Paul wrote.

For shoes, put on the peace that comes from the Good News, so that you will be fully prepared (Ephesians 6:15 NLT).

This speaks of Christians spreading the good news about Jesus Christ. Our job is to testify to the spiritually lost that there is forgiveness of sin in the Person of Jesus Christ. We are to be ready to go wherever He will send us. Those who do this are said to have "beautiful feet." Paul wrote the following words to the Romans.

And how shall they preach unless they are sent? As it is written: "How beautiful are the feet of those who preach the gospel of peace, who bring glad tidings of good things!" (Romans 10:15 NKJV).

The good news of Jesus needs to be shared with others. When we do this we are said to have "beautiful feet."

A SHIELD

When the wicked one attacks, God provides a shield for believers to thwart these attacks. Paul wrote.

> In addition to all this, take up the shield of faith, with which you can extinguish all the flaming arrows of the evil one (Ephesians 6:16 NIV).

When we are attacked with fear and doubt, we are to place our faith in God's promises. Indeed, He always prevails.

A HELMET

The Bible also speaks of armor that protects the head. It is called the "helmet of salvation." Scripture says.

> Take the helmet of salvation (Ephesians 6:17 NRSV).

The head speaks of knowledge. We need to understand that we have been given assurance of salvation; seeing that it is the God of the Bible who will carry us through.

While Satan wants to keep believers ignorant of these truths, and to keep us in continual doubt and bondage, Jesus wants to set us free. In fact, we are told the following about the freedom in Christ.

> Therefore if the Son sets you free, you really will be free (John 8:36 HCSB).

The Lord is in the business of setting people free. This is something that we need to understand.

THE SWORD OF THE SPIRIT

Scripture now speaks of an offensive weapon in the armor of the believer. We have a sword in our hand, the Word of God. Paul wrote.

Put on salvation as your helmet, and take the sword of the Spirit, which is the word of God (Ephesians 6:17 NLT).

The Word of God is our offensive weapon. The believer needs to understand how to use the Bible effectively when the attacks of the enemy come.

WE MUST MAINTAIN CONSTANT COMMUNICATION WITH GOD

We are also told to constantly be in prayer to God. Paul wrote to the Ephesians about this necessity. He put it this way.

With every prayer and petition, pray at all times in the Spirit, and to this end be alert, with all perseverance and requests for all the saints (Ephesians 6:18 NET).

Talking to God on a constant basis can help stop the progress of the devil. This is something believers need to do to advance spiritually.

Elsewhere we are commanded to pray unceasingly.

Pray without ceasing (1 Thessalonians 5:17 KJV).

Believers are to be constantly in prayer. This is a must.

10. WE NEED TO REALIZE WHOSE FAMILY WE ARE PART OF

The Bible speaks of two families of humanity. There are those who are the children of God, and those who are the children of the devil. Each human being belongs to one of these two families. There is no third group.

Those who are in the family of God have their lives molded after Him. Those who belong to the devil act like their spiritual father. Believers ought to realize which family they are a part of and they should act accordingly. The Bible says.

Because whatever has been born of God conquers the world. This is the victory that has conquered the world: our faith (1 John 5:4 HCSB).

Believers belong to God's forever family.

11. WE ARE TO REST IN GOD'S PROMISES

Finally, we need to rest in the promises of God. Satan has been overcome and the victory is ours! Paul wrote to the Corinthians.

> No temptation has overtaken you except what is common to humanity. God is faithful and He will not allow you to be tempted beyond what you are able, but with the temptation He will also provide a way of escape, so that you are able to bear it (1 Corinthians 10:13 HCSB).

There are no insurmountable problems for believers. The Lord always provides a remedy.

Paul wrote to the Philippians about the strength which Jesus Christ provides.

> For I can do everything with the help of Christ who gives me the strength I need (Philippians 4:13 NLT).

Jesus Christ can give us the strength to resist the devil. Therefore, we must fight the battle in His strength.

In sum, the Bible has indicated a number of ways in which believers in Jesus Christ can have victory over the devil. We would be wise to understand how victory can be achieved, as well as putting these truths into practice.

SUMMARY TO QUESTION 36
HOW CAN THE BELIEVER HAVE VICTORY OVER THE DEVIL? (EPHESIANS 6:12-18)

Jesus Christ has defeated the devil. The Bible makes it clear that victory is His. Those of us who have believed in Christ are also victorious. We win because He has won.

While the ultimate victory has been won, we still have to fight spiritual battles as long as we are here upon the earth. Therefore, we should desire to achieve earthly victories over the devil.

The Bible gives us a number of ways in which we can deal with the devil. Though the devil has been defeated, and eventually will be thrown into the lake of fire, he is still actively spreading evil. Christians need to understand who he is, and what he is able to do, while he is still active. As long as one looks to Jesus Christ, victory can be achieved. There are a number of things we can and should do.

For one thing, we must always remember that we do not have to sin. Sin is a choice that we make. However, we can flee from sin through the power of the Holy Spirit. This is really good news!

In addition, believers are said to be "in Christ." Consequently, as those who belong to Jesus Christ, we need to realize that the devil cannot harm us. We are protected by the One who has died for us.

We must recognize, however, in our dealings with the devil that we will have some spiritual victories, as well as some defeats. While we will eventually win the war, we may not win every battle. Yet victory is always possible.

To achieve victory there are a number of things we can and should do.

First, we need to know our enemy. This means having a biblical understanding of who the devil is, what he can do, and what he cannot do. This only comes from a study of Scripture.

We also need to know his methods. Scripture tells us some of the ways in which he works. Believers must, therefore, be able to spiritually discern what comes from the Lord, and what comes from the devil.

There is also the need to test the spirits. This means that we do not blindly believe everyone who claims to speak in the name of the Lord. We need to be active in doing this. Unfortunately, there will always be false prophets and counterfeit believers in the world.

Furthermore, Christians must actively be on guard against Satan and his attacks. We are to be watchful, to be ready at all times. Indeed, he is always actively seeking to devour us.

When Satan does attack we must resist. Indeed, we should not give in to his temptations. This calls for active participation on our part.

It is also extremely important that we know our weaknesses. Each of us has them. We should never pretend that we do not. Therefore, we should know the areas in which we are vulnerable and protect ourselves in these areas the best way in which we can.

Ultimately, we do not, and we cannot, fight the battle in our own strength. We can only resist Satan in the strength of the Lord.

Knowing our weaknesses, we do not want to put ourselves in a position where we can easily fail. We need to flee certain situations!

The Bible speaks of the spiritual weapons of warfare that we possess and we need to use them. They are there for us to win the battle. Victories are achievable when these weapons are employed.

Constant communication with the Lord can also help us in our battle against the devil. We should always be talking to Him, as well as letting Him constantly talk to us.

We must always realize whose family we belong to. It is the family of God. As His children we are under His care. He is always watching out for us. This is a comforting truth.

Furthermore, we need to live consistently with who we are, God's people. Indeed, we need to display to the world that we belong to Him. This means that we are to act differently than unbelievers in many situations. We should never compromise our belief or our behavior.

Above all, we must trust the promises of God and rest in them. By doing this we can have victory over Satan.

APPENDIX 1

Who Incited David To Number The Fighting Men Of Israel And Judah: God Or Satan? (2 Samuel 24:1, 1 Chronicles 21:1)

The Bible records an episode in the life of King David when he took an unwise census. This caused the Lord to harshly judge him and the people of Israel and Judah. However, in the two places in Scripture where this incident is recorded we find that the cause behind the numbering is different.

For example, in the book of Second Samuel, it is God who incited David to do this census.

> The Lord's anger again raged against Israel, and he incited David against them, saying, "Go count Israel and Judah" (2 Samuel 24:1 NET).

Yet, in the Book of First Chronicles the cause for numbering his people is said to be Satan.

> Satan rose up against Israel and incited David to take a census of Israel (1 Chronicles 21:1 NIV).

So which is it? Was it God or Satan who incited David to take this unwise census? How are we to understand what the Bible is telling us?

THE CONTEXT OF SECOND SAMUEL 24 AND FIRST CHRONICLES 21

To put this account into proper perspective we must first look at the historical background of this event as well as what takes place afterward.

The last four chapters in Second Samuel are generally viewed as an appendix to the book. They are placed there as a summation to the life and reign of King David but also as an introduction to the continuing story of the Lord dealing with His people as found in 1 and 2 Kings.

In fact, the account of the plague was placed in the final chapter in the book for a specific reason; it introduces the reader to the location of the future Temple.

Indeed, as soon as the location had been divinely pointed out, King David, as much as he was able, began preparations for its construction. The Book of First Chronicles, chapters 22-29, inform us to all that David did with a view to the building of this Temple. Therefore, the punishment of the nation of Israel, as recorded in Second Samuel 24, led to the construction of the temple as is documented in 1 and 2 Kings.

To sum up, the overall context of the message of Samuel, Kings, and Chronicles must be appreciated when we examine this particular episode in the life of David and the nation.

THE IMMEDIATE CONTEXT

With this in mind, let us look at the immediate context. Second Samuel 24 starts out by telling us that the anger of the Lord burned against Israel "again." We do not know the exact reason for the Lord's wrath against the people at this time. However, as on previous occasions, it must have stemmed from Israel's violation of some aspect of the Law of Moses.

To bring punishment to the people for this violation, we are told that the Lord incited David to conduct a census of the fighting men of Israel and Judah.

Earlier in Second Samuel, we discover that King David fought off two rebellions against his rule. One was from his own son Absalom (2 Samuel 15-17) while another came from a man named Sheba (2 Samuel 20:1-22).

It is possible that another threat had arisen. It is also conceivable that David was concerned about a future rebellion. Whatever the case may be, David chose to take a census of his fighting men.

Taking a census of the fighting men of Israel was something that had previously occurred. We read about this in the Book of Numbers.

> The Lord spoke to Moses in the tent of meeting in the Desert of Sinai on the first day of the second month of the second year after the Israelites came out of Egypt. He said: "Take a census of the whole Israelite community by their clans and families, listing every man by name, one by one. You and Aaron are to count according to their divisions all the men in Israel who are twenty years old or more and able to serve in the army" (Numbers 1:1-3 NIV).

Therefore, it was not something unique in the history of the nation to take a census that was limited to the fighting men.

WHY WAS THE LORD DISPLEASED WITH DAVID FOR TAKING THE CENSUS?

If this type of census was allowable under the Mosaic Law, then why was the Lord displeased with David for doing such a thing? Why did Joab, the commander of David's army, warn him about it?

As we delve deeper into what took place, we find that there are a number of reasons as to why this census brought about the wrath of God.

PROBLEM 1: DAVID ALONE INITIATED THE CENSUS TO COUNT THE FIGHTING MEN

The first problem with the census concerns David's role. While it is true that the Bible speaks of other occasions when the fighting men of

Israel were counted, it was always *God* who commanded that the census be taken. In this instance, the idea was not God's, but King David's and his alone. In fact, he did not seek that Lord at all about conducting this census.

Furthermore, the fact that David's census was limited to the fighting men angered the Lord. We read the following in Chronicles.

> David did not count the males twenty years old and under, for the Lord had promised to make Israel as numerous as the stars in the sky. Joab son of Zeruiah started to count the men but did not finish. God was angry with Israel because of this, so the number was not recorded in the scroll called The Annals of King David (1 Chronicles 27:23-24 NET).

While the Lord had promised to make the nation as numerous as the stars, David did not count those under the age of twenty. This omission infuriated the Lord.

In sum, taking a census of only the "fighting men" impugned the faithfulness of God. Indeed, this particular census was about how many soldiers David had at *his* disposal.

Therefore, David sinned by placing confidence in his large military force rather than in the Lord. In point of fact, it was the Lord, and the Lord alone, who had delivered him from his enemies in the past. Furthermore, God had promised to do so in the future. In this instance, David ignored the Lord as well as His previous divine interventions on behalf of the king.

PROBLEM 2: DAVID IGNORED THE LAW OF MOSES

There seems to be another reason as to why the Lord was angry with this entire episode; David disobeyed the law of Moses in his execution of the census. The Bible gives this command.

Then the Lord said to Moses, "When you take a census of the Israelites to count them, each one must pay the Lord a ransom for his life at the time he is counted. Then no plague will come on them when you number them. Each one who crosses over to those already counted is to give a half shekel, according to the sanctuary shekel, which weighs twenty gerahs. This half shekel is an offering to the Lord" (Exodus 30:11-12 NIV).

God warned that He would send a plague on the nation if they ignored the redemption money. There is no indication that David collected the money when he proceeded with his census.

Consequently, there were two issues here. First, David, without consulting the Lord, commanded that a census of the fighting men be taken. Second, the king did not order the people to pay the required money when the census was conducted. By not requiring the payment, David was violating the law of Moses.

OTHER POSSIBLY REASONS FOR THE LORD'S ANGER

Apart from these two seemingly obvious reasons as to why the Lord was angry at the census, there have been a number of other suggestions that commentators have made which could further explain why God's wrath came upon David and Israel.

THE PEOPLE HAD BECOME PROUD IN THEIR OWN ACCOMPLISHMENTS

Recall that Israel was a unique nation. Indeed, not only did it have a supernatural beginning with the birth of Isaac after his parents had aged beyond the childbearing years, their entire history was one of the Lord intervening on their behalf. Not only was He the One who miraculously brought them out of Egypt, we find that time and time again, the Lord had delivered them from their enemies.

Furthermore, the Lord continued to protect and provide for them to this particular moment in their history. However, it seems that the nation had forgotten all of this and began to take pride in their own accomplishments rather than what the Lord had done for them. In fact, they had forgotten why the Lord had created their nation; it was to be a testimony to Him, as well as a witness to the world of His power and His goodness. This prideful attitude in their own achievements is also what brought the anger of the Lord in this instance.

DAVID SEEMINGLY CHANGED THE METHOD OF FORMING ISRAEL'S ARMY

Another likely reason for the anger of the Lord concerned how David was changing the rules of the organization of Israel's army. The king wanted to have a standing army; an army at the ready. In other words, he wanted to create a military monarchy. This is not how the Lord had originally organized the nation or its fighting men. Therefore, the king, in changing the rules, was usurping God's authority.

This is why his commander Joab questioned David about taking this particular census. Though not a man of deep spiritual insight, he realized that David's act was sinful and could have serious consequences for the nation.

In sum, there were many reasons as to why this census of David was not only unwise, it was also contrary to the direct commands of God.

DAVID CONFESSES HIS SIN

After ten months into the census, the king recognized his sin.

> David was conscience-stricken after he had counted the fighting men, and he said to the Lord, "I have sinned greatly in what I have done. Now, Lord, I beg you, take away the guilt of your servant. I have done a very foolish thing" (2 Samuel 24:10 NIV).

This thing that David had done had displeased the Lord. Therefore, punishment was necessary. The Bible explains it this way.

> This command was also evil in the sight of God; so he punished Israel (1 Chronicles 21:7 NIV).

Though David wanted to take the blame alone, the people of Israel were also guilty.

After David felt regret for his folly, the prophet Gad then approached the king. He was informed that the Lord offered him to choose between three forms of punishment to come upon the people and the land.

> So Gad went to David and said to him, "Shall there come on you three years of famine in your land? Or three months of fleeing from your enemies while they pursue you? Or three days of plague in your land? Now then, think it over and decide how I should answer the one who sent me." David said to Gad, "I am in deep distress. Let us fall into the hands of the Lord, for his mercy is great; but do not let me fall into human hands" (2 Samuel 24:13,14 NIV).

Interestingly, each choice would lessen the number of people that the king had been so proud to count. David wisely decided to place himself and Israel under the mercy of the Lord.

After the plague killed some 70,000 people in the very first day, the Bible records the following took place.

> When the angel extended his hand to destroy Jerusalem, the Lord relented from his judgment. He told the angel who was killing the people, "That's enough! Stop now!" (Now the Lord's angel was near the threshing floor of Araunah the Jebusite) (2 Samuel 24:16 NET).

The Lord was truly merciful to Israel in general, and Jerusalem in particular. In fact, instead of three days, the punishment lasted only one day.

David then purchased the threshing floor of Araunah, the site where the plague stopped, and built an altar to the Lord there.

> David built an altar to the Lord there and sacrificed burnt offerings and fellowship offerings. Then the Lord answered his prayer in behalf of the land, and the plague on Israel was stopped (2 Samuel 24:25 NIV).

This would eventually be the site where the Temple would be built. As we mentioned, this episode sets the stage for the construction of the Temple and the future blessings that the Lord had is store for the people and the land.

QUESTIONS THAT NEED TO BE ANSWERED

This account does bring up several difficult questions which need to be answered. First, who was it that incited David to number his troops? Was it the Lord, as we read in First Samuel, or was it Satan, as is stated in Chronicles?

Second, why would the Lord Himself incite David to number the fighting men if it was contrary to His divine will? In fact, would not this put the Lord in the role as the Tempter?

Furthermore, how then could the king be blamed for his actions if he was incited by the Lord?

Finally, why should the people be punished for something the Lord initially caused David, and David alone, to do? Why punish them for David's sin?

These are some of the issues which need to be answered.

WAS IT SATAN OR A HUMAN ADVERSARY WHO INCITED DAVID?

Before we attempt to sort out the differences between the two accounts, and answer these questions, there is something that we must note. The writer of Chronicles wrote that "Satan" moved David to take the census. As we have mentioned earlier in this book, the Hebrew word *satan* has a number of meanings. It can be a proper name, or it can refer to a personage who is an adversary of someone else.

Therefore, it is possible that this verse in Chronicles refers to the created being who became "the devil." However, it is also possible that a human adversary is in view. This is reflected in a number of English translations. For example, the NET Bible renders the verse as follows.

> An adversary opposed Israel, inciting David to count how many warriors Israel had (1 Chronicles 21:1 NET).

This understanding of the word would likely mean that some human adversary, who was opposed to David, was the person who incited him to number his troops. As we earlier mentioned, it could have been some threat from a neighboring enemy.

GOD WAS ULTIMATELY RESPONSIBLE

While the writer of Samuel said God was responsible for inciting David and the Chronicler said Satan, or a human adversary, was responsible, at the end of the day both were true. It seems that the Lord used an adversary to bring judgment on the objects of His anger; David and the nation of Israel.

Therefore, we could discover three or four levels of causality in this episode. The ultimate cause was the Lord Himself who, for some reason, was angry at His people. However, He used Satan, or some hostile human instrument, to incite David to sin against the Lord by conducting this census.

DOES THIS MEAN GOD CAUSES PEOPLE TO SIN?

We are told that in order to bring judgment against the nation of Israel, the Lord "incited David" to "take a census of Israel and Judah."

This brings up an often-asked question: if the Lord is the One who incited David to number the people, then doesn't that mean that He is responsible for David's sin? How can David be blamed if the Lord orchestrated the entire episode?

To answer this question, a number of things must be mentioned. First, the fact that Second Samuel attributes the action to the Lord does not contradict what we read in First Chronicles. Indeed, these passages are a reflection of the understanding that the God of Israel is the Lord of the entire universe! In fact, He exercises His dominion over all personages that exist. This includes those in heaven as well as those upon the earth. The psalmist recognized this and wrote the following.

> For you, O Lord, are the sovereign king a over the whole earth; you are elevated high above all gods (Psalm 97:9 NET).

We read the same thing in the New Testament.

> This power he [God] exercised in Christ when he raised him from the dead and seated him at his right hand in the heavenly realms far above every rule and authority and power and dominion and every name that is named, not only in this age but also in the one to come (Ephesians 1:20,21 NET).

As the One who is in control of the entire universe, we find that the Lord, at times, allocates, or allows, power to other beings to do His bidding. This may include ungodly humans as in the case with the Babylonians. We read about this in the book of Habakkuk.

> Look, I am about to empower the Babylonians, that ruthless and greedy nation. They sweep across the surface of the earth, seizing dwelling places that do not belong to them (Habakkuk 1:6 NET).

The evil Babylonians were used as an instrument of God's judgment against Israel.

We also find that the Lord may send a supernatural influence upon people to bring about His desired results. We read about this in the New Testament.

> The arrival of the lawless one will be by Satan's working with all kinds of miracles and signs and false wonders, and with every kind of evil deception directed against those who are perishing, because they found no place in their hearts for the truth so as to be saved. Consequently God sends on them a deluding influence so that they will believe what is false (2 Thessalonians 2:9-11 NET).

Therefore, in limited ways and at certain times, the Lord does indeed do such things to bring about His desired goals.

As we have stressed, the Lord used some type of adversary, whether human or superhuman, to incite David. Yet while David could have resisted this incitement, he did not. In fact, we find that he confessed his own wrongdoing. Ultimately, the blame rests entirely upon David. While there were indeed forces which influenced him, at the end of the day he made his own choice.

GOD DOES NOT TEMPT PEOPLE TO SIN

We know from the Bible that the Lord does not tempt humans to sin. The Book of James states the following.

> When tempted, no one should say, "God is tempting me." For God cannot be tempted by evil, nor does he tempt anyone; but each person is tempted when they are dragged away by their own evil desire and enticed (James 1:13,14 NIV).

Scripture is clear on this fact; God does not tempt people to sin. In this particular instance, it was the previous sin of David, as well as the sin of the people of Israel, that caused the Lord to create the circumstances for David's folly. While some adversary did incite David, he could have resisted it. In other words, a census was not his only option. David could have sought the Lord and His guidance about what to do with this threat. But he did not. Instead, the king took it upon himself to remedy the situation by ordering a census of his fighting men as well as creating a standing army to deal with his enemies.

It seems the people of Israel also went along with this prideful foolishness. This is what caused the plague to come upon them.

GOD GAVE DAVID TIME TO REPENT

There is something else which should be appreciated. David's sin was not something that happened on the spur of the moment. Indeed, this was a prideful calculated rebellion against the Lord. In fact, it was ten months into the census before David felt remorse for what he had done. God had given the king that much time to consider his actions and to repent of his sin. Recall Joab had initially counseled the king against conducting this census. However, David would not listen to anyone. In other words, he deliberately persisted in his sin for almost a year.

SOME FINAL CONCLUSIONS

As we consider the totality of what took place, it is of the utmost importance to remember that this punishment was sent as a result of some sin for which Israel, as a people, were guilty. While it is true that the direct cause was the prideful and carnal confidence of David, his state of mind also reflected the state of mind of the people. This allowed some adversary to incite the king, with apparently the full consent of the people, to conduct this unneeded census.

This also illustrates an Old Testament principle; the solidarity of a people with their rulers. In other words, they acted and thought as one. This seems to be what was taking place here. Indeed, the prideful arrogance of the nation was from the king on down.

In sum, God used certain circumstances to punish the king and his people for their sin against him. Neither the king nor his people were blameless. Furthermore, though given time to repent, David continued in his rebellion. In addition, we find no outpouring of grief or conviction of sin among the people in the conducting of the census. These circumstances caused the Lord to send the plague upon Israel.

However there is good news! This episode of human sin, as well as God's mercy, will provide the context for the continuing story of the Lord's dealings with His people, as found in 1 and 2 Kings. In fact, the readers will discover that the Lord will use this plague to mark the spot where His holy Temple will be built! They will be also be introduced to the actual builder of the Temple, Solomon.

In other words, the Lord has not set aside the nation of Israel. Indeed, the land and the people will continue to be under His blessing. Consequently, the end result of this sordid episode will be for the redemption of the people of Israel.

SUMMARY TO APPENDIX 1
WHO INCITED DAVID TO NUMBER THE FIGHTING MEN OF ISRAEL AND JUDAH: GOD OR SATAN? (2 SAMUEL 24:1, 1 CHRONICLES 21:1)

The two accounts of King David taking a census of the fighting men of Israel bring up a number of questions. This includes who actually incited David to conduct the census. In addition, if the Lord was ultimately behind David's actions, then how could the king be personally blamed for it? Why then was the nation punished for something which the Lord initiated?

We find that David's numbering of Israel and Judah was an act of pride. Indeed, he was placing his faith in his military might rather than in the Lord. Though Joab his commander questioned him about this needless census, prideful David nevertheless went about conducting it.

While the Lord was indeed behind the inciting of King David, He used some type of adversary, either Satan or a human enemy, to stir up the king.

Yet we must remember that David did not have to respond to the incitement by conducting a census. He should have sought the Lord on the matter, but did not. This reflected not only his prideful state but also that of the people of Israel at that time. In fact, the entire account begins with the Lord being angry at the people for some unspoken sin.

The conducting of the census, with the cooperation of the people, caused the Lord to send a plague upon the nation. Mercifully, the Lord stopped His punishment when it had reached the city of Jerusalem.

In fact, the very place where the plague stopped would be the location where the first Temple would eventually be built. Therefore, the story of the sin of David and the people of Israel, along with the ensuing plague, set the stage for one of the greatest accomplishments in the history of the nation; the building of a Temple in which the Lord would dwell with His people in a special way.

Consequently, as we discover in the books of 1 and 2 Kings, the Lord was not finished with the nation of Israel. In fact, His blessing would still be upon them as well as upon the Promised Land. This is one of the many lessons that we learn from looking at this entire episode.

About The Author

Don Stewart is a graduate of Biola University and Talbot Theological Seminary (with the highest honors).

Don is a best-selling and award-winning author having authored, or co-authored, over seventy books. This includes the best-selling *Answers to Tough Questions*, with Josh McDowell, as well as the award-winning book *Family Handbook of Christian Knowledge: The Bible*. His various writings have been translated into over thirty different languages and have sold over a million copies.

Don has traveled around the world proclaiming and defending the historic Christian faith. He has also taught both Hebrew and Greek at the undergraduate level and Greek at the graduate level.

63665968R00154

Made in the USA
Charleston, SC
10 November 2016